Goodnight Children, Everywhere

Goodnight Children, Everywhere

Lost Voices of Evacuees

MONICA B. MORRIS

First published 2009

The History Press
The Mill, Brimscombe Port
Stroud, Gloucestershire, GL5 2QG
www.thehistorypress.co.uk

British Library Cataloguing in Publication Data.
A catalogue record for this book is available from the British Library.

ISBN 978 0 7524 5282 1

Typesetting and origination by The History Press
Printed in Great Britain

Contents

Acknowledgements

A book is never solely the work of one person. I am indebted, first, to Diz White, my friend and colleague, author of *Haunted Cotswolds* and *Haunted Cheltenham*, whose cheerful enthusiasm kept my nose to the grindstone – or, rather, my fingers on the computer keys – even when I would rather have gone fishing. Thanks, also, to my walking buddy, Maureen Bailey, with whom I shared many of my ideas when we were hiking in Bronson Canyon, and who always asked pertinent and thought-provoking questions.

Without the men and women who sat patiently and told me their stories, I would have no book. Thank you all; I am eternally grateful. And to Nicola Guy of The History Press goes my appreciation for her optimism and advocacy; you are a treasure.

Finally, to my husband: it isn't easy being married to a writer! You may hope that she is simply sharing a meal with you as you look at her across the dining table, but you know she is editing passages and juggling facts and figures, and mixing moonbeams and metaphors in her head! So thank you Clark, for your understanding, patience and encouragement.

Images

Many thanks to the Associated Press, the Imperial War Museum and Diz White for allowing the reproduction of the images in this book.

Note: Some names have been changed or omitted for protection of individual privacy.

Introduction

The beginning of September 1939 saw a unique event in Britain's history.

Never before had millions of children – close to a million just from London alone – been moved from the cities to the countryside in the space of three or four days, and without a single accident or casualty. 'Operation Pied Piper', as this Government Evacuation Scheme was dubbed, has been described as the largest, best-prepared and most minutely organized movement of mothers and infants, schoolchildren and others ever conceived in peacetime. No one has ever seen anything quite comparable. And although this was not the only time during that era that the children were transported from place to place – there was another evacuation, 'Operation Trickle', in October 1940 to take the children away from the Blitz, and still another, 'Operation Rivulet', in the autumn of 1944 – it was the one at the onset of the war that seared minds and spirits most; it lingers still in the memory.

Most of the people telling their stories in this book make some mention of their parents seeing them off on the buses – or deliberately not seeing them off. Some, including myself, claim that parents had been told to stay away from schools and other embarkation points – to avoid displays of emotion that might slow down the process. Others mention that their mothers walked with them to school and helped them to carry their luggage. I wondered, therefore, if there had been any official policy and learned that while parents were generally not to be allowed on railway platforms, head teachers appear to have made individual decisions about the parents of their students making their farewells at their schools.

Margaret Gaskin, in her book *Blitz,* tells of the headmistress of the London County Council's Stoke Newington Junior and Infant Schools who had called a joint emergency meeting for parents at the start of September 1939, on the eve of the children's departure. One teacher recalls how solemn it was in the school hall, packed with grim-faced parents who listened in silence as the headmistress ran through the drill for the following day.

'You will want to see them off,' she began. She then gently requested that they stand around the playground walls and wave the children off cheerfully as they marched out. 'Shed your tears after they have left,' she urged. She also reminded them to appreciate the sacrifices that the teachers were making. They, too, were leaving their homes and their families to shoulder the serious responsibility of looking after other people's children. Her advice was followed to the letter. The parents who came to the school smiled through their anguish and the children went off cheerfully. As the children left the playground and climbed onto the buses, the parents all waved and so did the children. 'It was a most moving sight,' the teacher continued. 'the children and their parents showed great courage. The only tears I saw shed that day were those of the young bus driver who… wept all the way to Finsbury Park where we disembarked.'

That parents were so cooperative as their children were taken away to unknown destinations, perhaps never to be seen again, is testament to the trust that parents put in the school staff and in the government. Further, they had been persuaded that their sacrifice was warranted. This mass exodus of September 1939 had been in the planning since the early 1930s. It was anticipated that the bombing would begin as soon as war was declared, and there were predictions of as many as 4 million civilian casualties in London alone.

As early as 1922, after the air threat from Zeppelins, Lord Balfour had suggested that 'the capital of the Empire would be subjected to unremitting bombardment of a kind that no other city… has ever had to endure…' It was felt that the inferior housing of poor people would be the first to collapse and as many children from the cities, especially from the East End of London, lived in sub-standard dwellings, it was vital to get them into safer areas as quickly as possible. The rich were thought to be able to fend for themselves. They could leave the cities as families or they could send their children to America or to the colonies.

The estimates of casualties, as it turned out, was something of an exaggeration. According to Richard M. Titmuss, from the onset of the Blitz on 7 September 1940 when the bombing began, until 1 January 1941, some 13,596 Londoners were killed and 18,378 were severely injured. On 10/11 May 1941, a further 6,487 were killed and 7,641 were injured. These are horrifyingly large numbers but they are far from the many millions of casualties estimated.

Further, the bombardment did not begin with the declaration of war, as was predicted. The Blitz began a whole year later, in September 1940, and during this period, known as 'the phoney war,' when 'nothing was happening', thousands of homesick children had returned to the cities. As early as November 1939, more than 6,000 children a week were returning to London alone, and by the summer of 1940, half of all that city's children were home – I was one of them – and their parents had to be persuaded to send them away again.

Government officials were clearly concerned by this turn of events and struggled to find reasons and remedies. One of the first suggestions by the Public Health Propaganda Office was that a letter 'in simplest language', signed by the Queen, should be sent to every mother and father whose child had been evacuated. It was found impractical that the Queen should send this letter, but the language of the intended message – and the commentary by the compilers of the letter – are instructive. They wrote, 'This letter is specially designed for simple people. We think officialese would spoil it.'

The proposed letter read:

Christmas is at hand, and for the first time in your lives many of you are not able to have your children all around you.

I know how you are feeling, but I want you to be very brave and to put up with this for the sake of our country and for the sake of your boys and girls.

The country will need them in the days to come, to build up once more a happy land.

You may say that there does not seem much risk from air raids. But we do not know for certain. Even before you read this letter, we may have been called upon to suffer, and because the King and I are not taking the risks with our children, I ask you not to take the risk with yours.

I beg you to leave the children in the country til it is safe to bring them home. We shall all be told when that moment arrives.

Other plans to keep the children in the country included posters on buses and slogans flashed on screens in cinemas, 'Children are safer in the country, leave them there!' One of the Ministry of Health posters shows an outline of Adolf Hitler whispering in the ear of a mother who is visiting her children in the country. 'Take them Back! Take them Back! Take them Back!' he urges the mother, who is clearly reflecting on the issue. 'Don't Do It, Mother!' – the caption positively screams. 'Leave your Children in the Safer Areas!'. The *News of the World* published articles encouraging parents not to bring their children home. J.B. Priestley wrote such an article in the *News Chronicle*; E.M. Delafield wrote similar pieces in *Tit Bits, House and Country*, and *St Martin's Review*; features were aired on the radio, and an evacuation film was hastily produced, all in an effort towards 'systematic propaganda.' Only when the heavy bombardment began was there another exodus to the country.

Some seventy years have passed since the evacuation of the children who are now in their mid-seventies to their mid-eighties. Like the soldiers of the Second World War, they will disappear before long and their memories will disappear with them.

For this reason, I have been collecting the stories of the now-adult Second World War evacuees. Mine is a 'snowball' or 'contingency' sample of interviewees. It is made up of people who answered my advertisements seeking anyone who had been an evacuee in 1939. I interviewed and tape-recorded each of them for several hours, encouraging them to talk freely about everything they remembered of their experiences. As it turned out, almost all my respondents came from London or from the south of England, and many of them had migrated from England as adults and made their homes abroad. As well as face-to-face interviews with the now adult evacuees, I also spent many hours in research at the Imperial War Museum in London and at various Record Offices, collecting archive material of the time. This included some letters from mothers complaining about their children's billets, and from foster homes complaining of the children being dirty, or ill-behaved. Some of the archives had been closed to the public and to researchers until the 1970s and some until the 1980s, and contained information from the Ministry of Education and the Ministry of Housing and local government.

As usually happens in any study of this kind, patterns soon began to emerge from the stories; certain common themes ran through the tapes like sombre or brightly-coloured threads. Many of the children were placed with good people who treated them well, but not all were as fortunate. The well-to-do 'hosts' often relegated their evacuees to the 'downstairs' to live with the servants. Others picked older, stronger children to work as unpaid maids or farm hands. Some were malnourished and otherwise ill-treated. Some were moved from billet to billet, rejected by household after household. Schooling, too, was sparse, even non-existent, many of the evacuees having to share the facilities with the village children, further adding to the resentment of some villagers towards the interlopers.

Bias against the evacuees was both religious and class-based, and suspicion and dislike were exacerbated when children and hosts were mismatched. Records show that many Catholic youngsters, for example, were sent to regions where no Catholic families lived and were made to attend Protestant services. Thousands of Jewish children from London's East End were faced with anti-Semitism, both direct and unwitting, for the first time in their lives. To some villagers, Jews personified the Devil. To others, they were merely curiosities, alien creatures with strange and 'foreign' dietary requirements. Further, in a society with sharp class distinctions, poor city children were thought to be badly reared and dirty, a pre-judgment supported by the large numbers of evacuees who became bed-wetters and were sometimes punished for this 'disgusting' behaviour – behaviour undoubtedly prompted by the trauma of separation from family and familiar surroundings.

So, while the transportation of the children to safety was undeniably successful, and although a great many children found much joy in their adopted homes – in the understanding and kindness of their temporary families, and in the pleasure they found in the countryside – the problems that would later emerge were unanticipated, hence little preparation had been made to address them. Accusations have been levelled against the controversial Sir John Anderson, Lord Privy Seal in Neville Chamberlain's Cabinet and the man in charge of the evacuation. He is described by David Prest, in a BBC Online article published in 1999, as 'a cold, inhuman character with little understanding of the emotional upheaval that might be created by the evacuation.' Elsewhere, Anderson was viewed as the man who 'expertly worked out plans for three million evacuees.' Clearly, the first task of the evacuation was to remove the most vulnerable civilians from danger, and in this the plan succeeded.

My own experiences as an evacuee from London form a through-line to this book: three separate chapters, interspersed with the stories of several other evacuees, and with commentary about specific aspects of the evacuation and its planning. The title, *Goodnight Children, Everywhere* is, of course, from the song of that name that was heard throughout the war. It was sung by Vera Lynn, who was also known as 'The Forces' Sweetheart' for songs with sentiments pertinent to the longings of servicemen and women away from home. Listening to Vera Lynn's song for the children now still brings the hint of a tear to the eye, a lump to the throat – and not a little retrospective distress, for the message is mixed. While the words ask the children to be brave, 'Rest your head upon your pillow/Don't be kid or a weeping willow,' the sob in Ms Lynn's voice implies that she, like the children, is holding back her tears, trying to keep a stiff upper lip while she sings, 'Your Mummy thinks of you tonight.' Hearing this, any homesick little boy or girl might well have poured tears of grief into that pillow – as did I, all those years ago.

One

My Story, Part One

It was a glorious summer, the summer of 1939. City children all over London played in the streets and alleys. Perhaps there wouldn't be a war, but the authorities seemed to be getting ready. Gas masks were issued to everyone, even special little ones for us children. I tried mine on, adjusting the straps at the back so it fitted tightly below my chin. It smelled of rubber and soon got so hot inside that the celluloid eyepiece steamed up and I couldn't see out. I thought I was suffocating and frantically ripped the ugly thing from my face.

We were supposed to carry our gas masks at all times. I volunteered to deliver the containers in the neighbourhood, thrilled to be knocking on doors and showing people how to assemble the flat pieces of cardboard so they were transformed into perfect cubes with lid flaps that tucked inside.

'You see those marks on the side?' I said, revelling at ten years old in my official position as instructor. 'You make holes there and thread string through. See?' Cardboard wouldn't last long in the rainy weather, though, and people soon made covers of oil-cloth for their boxes and, before long, several kinds of cases appeared in the shops, some cube-shaped, some slim and shapely, contoured closely to the lines of the gas masks. Some were made of brocade and silk, for evening wear. Fashion accessories.

We kids didn't think about war; the evacuation drills were just a summer diversion. A game. Crowds of excited youngsters gathered in the schoolyards, gas masks slung over their shoulders, twists of barley sugar – to prevent travel sickness – clutched in their hands.

Then the game of evacuation became real. I half-walked, half-ran to my school – Benthal Road, in Stoke Newington – hampered by my heavy luggage, my gas mask in its cardboard box bouncing on my hip as I walked. I put the case down from time to time to sweep the long tendrils of my hair back over my forehead and clip them more firmly into place. At the school gate, my case was taken from me, the strings of a cardboard label bearing the name of my school were threaded through a buttonhole on my coat and I was steered to the end of one of several long lines of children stretching across the playground. Where were my classmates? I looked around for familiar faces, standing on the tips of my toes, straining to see over the heads of the taller children. 'Stay in your lines, boys and girls!' a voice ordered loudly. 'Each line will march out in turn, starting from this corner!'

We moved briskly across the schoolyard in single file, through the side gate and into the street where a line of double-decker buses awaited us. Double-deckers in that narrow street! Buses never ran there. I thought it was great fun. I wished I still had my barley sugar, but I had eaten it long ago, savouring its sweetness as it splintered in my mouth. I climbed up the steps of the first bus and onto the front seat where I could see right over the brick wall of the schoolyard to the hundreds of children snaking across the asphalt. Over near the lavatories, piles of suitcases, secured with bits of string and old trousers' belts awaited collection. Outside the school gates, edging the road, a small group of grown-ups waited, come to watch the children go. Glancing down, I was surprised to see my mother among them. She had already hugged me goodbye at home, just like an ordinary school day, except that it was a Saturday and I supposed she didn't have to go into work.

I banged on the window, shouting 'Mummy! Mum! I'm up here!' until she saw me. She tried to smile but she could manage only a kind of grimace, her lips barely parting across her teeth in a valiant effort to appear cheerful. Our parents were not told where we were going and they had no assurance that they would ever see us again. I learned later that parents had been asked to stay away from departure points, presumably so that the operation would proceed smoothly, without emotional outbursts and delays.

As soon as every seat was taken, the bus creaked away from the curb and along the small side street, swinging wide at the corner. I looked back. My mother was still there, watching the bus leave. She was waving, although I knew I was no longer in her view.

It was a secret where we were going. Even the teachers didn't know. Or, if they knew, they weren't saying. I quite liked secrets because they were usually about nice surprises. The buses emptied at the mainline railways station and, directed by teachers and other helpers, we all filed through the corridors, into the great booking hall, and then along the platforms onto the waiting trains. My attention was so diverted by the bookstalls with their piles of coloured magazines, and the little shops that sold marvellous, mouth-watering fruit, and the machines that dispensed penny bars of Nestles, and the crowds, and the porters with their peaked caps rushing by with carts piled high with luggage and mailbags, that it was some moments before I realised that my group was gone. I ran along the platforms, looking for people wearing labels like mine. No one. I darted out through the barrier, back into the main hall, along one white tiled corridor and into another, longer corridor. Perhaps I could find out where the buses were coming in and start all over again. The passageways were labyrinthine, twisting and weaving, one into another. There seemed no way out. I was hot and out of breath; I couldn't tell how long I had been running.

'She's got no fear!' my mother constantly complained of me. 'A fearless little tomboy, that's what she is!' It was easy to be without fear when Mum and Dad and my brother were close by, and neighbours and friends. Torn from my small safe world, I was no braver than any other ten-year-old.

'Mummy!' I began to sob softly, almost experimentally. 'Mummy! I want you!' Then the tears flooded hot down my cheeks; I rubbed at them with my fists, ashamed to be crying, a big girl like me. The inside of my chest felt bruised from the effort to control the sobs. I groped around in the pocket where my mother sometimes secured a handkerchief with a safety pin. Nothing there. I swiped at my face with the back of my arm.

'What's this, then?' the porter leaned down. 'Lost, is it, ducks?' He scanned my label, grabbed my hand, and led me back into the main hall, gently joking, and poking fun at a big girl like me getting lost. 'Pretty young ladies with pretty blue eyes should never cry,' he chided, so by the time I was reunited with my group, I was laughing and the tears had dried. It hadn't been so long, after all. My line was just beginning to board the train.

The journey took many hours, although the distance was not great. The train rattled through the outskirts of London and into the green countryside where telegraph poles flashed by with rhythmic regularity. It travelled through open fields, past cows and sheep and banks of trees already losing their leaves. It raced through small villages and medium-sized towns and station after station without stopping.

We all cheered when the train finally drew to a halt. There, on the platform of a quiet country station, far from the main arteries of the railway system, plates of sandwiches and half-pint bottles of milk were set out on long trestle tables and kindly women in flowered aprons were there to serve us. Not far from the food, temporary toilets awaited – galvanized buckets sitting in a row behind canvas flaps.

Less lively now than at the start of the journey, we all climbed back onto the train with only a little pushing and shoving. We sat more sedately than before, some of the younger children falling asleep, their heads rocking with the rolling rhythm, their eyes jerking open as the train clattered across the points, their lids soon drooping once more. There was a timelessness about the day. Was it morning still? Or afternoon? Once again, the train pulled into a station, a big one this time, and stopped. Peterborough, someone said. Again, we children left the carriages, some leaping daringly onto the platform, the smaller ones needing help down the steep steps. Again, we formed lines and waited for instructions.

'Is this where we're stayin'?'

''Ow far are we from 'ome?'

''Undreds of miles, I betcha!'

'No. 'Tain' as far as that.'

'Sir! Sir! Where is this place?'

'Northamptonshire,' a passing teacher called back.

Northamptonshire? Where was that? It could just as well have been Nottingham, or Norfolk, or Nova Scotia. The lines of children streamed out of the station into the sunny, busy street and onto buses that waited, panting, with their engines running. The buses swung through the town, past crowds of Saturday afternoon shoppers standing by the kerbside gawking into the loaded vehicles, and out to where new suburbs of small brick bungalows fingered their way into the countryside. Paston. The ride ended but the day was not over. Herded off the buses and into the hall of the local school, we children, now reunited with our few belongings, waited to be collected. The noise of excited chatter, of children chasing after each other, the shrill shouting, the occasional weary sobs, rose and fell, rose and fell, orchestrated by teachers' periodic urgings for 'Quiet! Please!'

Anxious, I waited as one by one boys and girls were chosen and taken away. It was almost as though we were for sale. Customers came in, a few at a time, looked around, even pointed, and bore their choices home. It looked as though brothers and sisters were supposed to be kept together because sometimes two children went off, hand in hand, with the same shopper. I wished my brother were with me so I would have someone's hand to hold but he, nearly grown up at fifteen, had refused to be evacuated with the children. In so doing, he'd had to leave his prestigious private school, relinquishing his scholarship and thereby closing off any opportunities he might have had for higher education.

The hall gradually emptied of children and luggage and hustle and bustle and noise. The sun had long ago set; it was night and no one had picked me. The only child remaining, I waited, tired beyond tears, in the now silent hall.

'Don't you worry, duck!' The volunteer's voice echoed, even though she spoke quietly and gently. 'Someone'll come for you soon. They're just going through the lists again to see if they can find you a billet.'

An hour passed. Then another. Sitting on the dusty floor, I slowly slid down, fast asleep, my head resting on the edge of my suitcase, cushioned by my right arm; the other arm was flung over my old, threadbare Teddy, unearthed from my suitcase, lying close to me on the scuffed parquet floor. I slept until a pleasant woman gently woke me and walked me to her home.

So many people I later interviewed referred to the selection process as the 'cattle market' and so many, like myself, recall being 'left to the last' that the event seems to have left a scar on the collective psyche, a lasting sense of humiliation. Most of us were, after all, poorly dressed and the journey had left us tired, untidy, and streaked with grime.

'You can call me Mummy, if you like, the same as my girls do', Mrs Brown suggested as she steered me through the deserted, moon-lit streets. Sensitive to my lack of response, she quickly amended, 'Or Aunty Doll, if you'd rather.'

The distance from the Paston school to the Brown's bungalow was barely half a mile. Under other circumstances I would have skipped and hopped and jumped and asked questions and volunteered information. Not here, though, not with this woman, this stranger, who seemed to think she could be my Mummy, just for saying. Instead I was quiet, initiating no conversation, answering only when necessary. The day had drained me of curiosity, too weary to notice much about the neighbourhood, except for the big old trees whose branches formed a canopy over our heads. I moved slowly, dragging my feet alongside Mrs Brown, gripping my Teddy tightly under my left arm, my right hand holding the straps of my gas mask that bumped on my right hip as I walked. Mrs Brown carried my suitcase easily and it hung between us like a small barrier.

Only much later did Dolly Brown tell me that she hadn't wanted to take an evacuee. She had enough to do, she said, caring for her own family, without the added responsibility of some London child, some cockney child, perhaps some slum child. Yet, there was the spare room and it did seem selfish, if not downright unpatriotic, not to offer.

'Leave me to the last, I told the man,' she said. 'If there aren't enough billets, I'll take one little girl. Otherwise, I'd rather not.' So she knew who was knocking that evening of 2 September. Only officials and strangers came to the front door. Everyone else came to the kitchen. They needed a place for a girl of ten, they said. Ten. The same age as her Colleen.

'When I saw that poor kid lying there on the floor, Bert, with her tangled hair all over her face and her coat all twisted and bunched up round her waist, I felt really terrible,' she had admitted to her husband that night, she told me. 'She could be ours, I kept thinking. She could be our girl left all those hours before anyone cared enough to come for her. All alone. Tired out. Poor little mite.'

Breakfast at the Brown's that next morning was a leisurely affair with bacon, eggs, tomatoes and triangles of bread fried in bacon fat, and lively chatter to which even the taciturn Bert Brown contributed a few words. After a good night's sleep, the events of the previous day almost receded into the mists of memory as I cleaned my plate, wiping up the delicious drops of bacon grease with a chunk of bread. We never had bacon at home. I knew my mother did not keep a kosher kitchen, the way some of my friends' mothers did, although there were some forbidden things like shrimps and winkles that made her shudder delicately if anyone as much as mentioned them. She didn't cook bacon out of respect for the two families who shared the house with us, the Schmidts one floor below us and the Portnoys in the basement. The odour was unmistakable.

'The Chief Rabbi says Jewish evacuees should eat whatever they are given.' I repeated to the Browns what I had heard the day before as I picked up the last piece of fried bread on my plate, crunching it with pleasure, licking away the last droplet of bacon fat from my lower lip.

'What's a Jew?' seven-year-old Merle asked. 'Do I know any?'
Dolly Brown nodded towards me. 'There's one,' she answered simply. 'See, she's no different from anyone else.'

Both Merle and Colleen, her older sister, stared at me with unabashed curiosity, the two pairs of dark brown eyes open and unblinking. I looked back at them, not sure whether to smile at their serious faces.

'Stop it, you sillies!' Doll laughed. 'Anyone'd think she had horns growing out of her head!'

I laughed, too. Fancy not knowing any Jews, I knew hardly anyone who wasn't a Jew. Some of them were very religious, observing all the holidays, the men wearing their hats all the time – even in the bath, my Dad joked – but most were like my family; they knew they were Jews but they didn't think about it much.

After breakfast, Mr Brown – Uncle Bert – switched on the wireless so we could all listen to the Prime Minister's announcement.

'I am speaking to you from the Cabinet Room of Ten Downing Street,' Mr Chamberlain began, sounding serious, even sad. 'This morning the British Ambassador in Berlin handed the German government a final note stating that unless we heard from them by eleven o'clock that they were prepared to withdraw their troops from Poland, a state of war would exist between us. I have to tell you now that no such undertaking has been received and that, consequently, we are at war with Germany.'

I didn't really understand the importance of the announcement or why Aunty Doll suddenly put her arms around each of us three little girls in turn and hugged us tightly to her breast.

Two Sisters: Irene S. and Phyllis B.

Irene's Story

Irene was thirteen-and-a-half years old when she boarded the bus at the school in Newington Green, Islington, on the morning of 2 September 1939. She was holding on tightly to her seven-year-old sister's hand, keenly aware of her responsibility for the younger child's safety. Their mother, recently widowed, had walked with them and another child, their friend, to the school. 'My mother helped us with our suitcases. We had been told to bring luggage for a limited time – no one knew how long we were expected to be away – and we had to carry our gas masks, of course. My mother had put them in canvas bags to protect them. Our parents were told not to come to the station, so we had to say our goodbyes as we climbed on the bus.' Her brow furrowed as she thought about that parting. 'We had absolutely no idea where we were going and, even on the train we couldn't tell what towns we were going through because all the railway station signs had been taken down, but I think we went from Canonbury Station. We were on our way to Hemel Hempstead in Hertfordshire. Can you imagine! It was all of twenty-five miles from central London. You have to ask how safe the authorities thought we would be if or when the bombs started raining down on London! I think we were on the train for less than an hour, in spite of several stops along the way. And then we couldn't tell where we were when we arrived. We had to ask our teacher. Oh, and I do remember the boys and girls were segregated; we were evacuated in segregated age groups.'

'What happened to you once you arrived at Hemel Hempstead?' I asked, *'and how were you assigned to a billet?'*

'We were taken in a conveyance – I think it was a bus or a coach – from the station to the village of Boxmore, a suburb of Hemel Hempstead. We all walked to a fairground and we had to wait there in groups and people would come along and select whoever they wanted to take home as evacuees. We waited there for a long time, as children all around us were taken away.'

'How did you feel about being selected?'

'I remember very well being rather concerned. I was sensitive about who might pick us because we were Jewish at a time when – and we were very much aware of it – Oswald Mosley, the leader of the British Union of Fascists, had been marching through the East End of London, denouncing Jews, spreading anti-Semitic feeling. I knew there were going to be problems, there was most likely going to be a war, and I accepted the situation. And as for being chosen – I remember it as a kind of a market, in a way.'

'Who picked you and your little sister?' I asked.

'They were a Mr and Mrs Marlowe, and they picked my sister, myself, and my friend. Three of us. They took us in their big car to their house in Featherbed Lane. They were high-class Spanish/Portuguese people, and my friend and I were relieved that they were Jewish and we wouldn't have to worry on that score. Their beautiful country house was in a very upper class neighbourhood. The house was called 'The Beehive' and it was the kind of home that I had never seen in my life. It was in its own extensive grounds with a croquet court, an orchard, a nuttery…' She savoured the word, and repeated it. 'A nuttery, a rose garden, and a tennis court. It was quite a big house – not a mansion but it was what we would call a country residence. And the people led us from the car into their house and the first thing they did was to show us our bedrooms. I think they gave us one big bedroom for the three of us. Upstairs, I believe it was. It was quite lovely. And they straight away showed us where the bathroom was and said we should take baths. I don't know what they expected us to be like. You know, we came from poor but decent, well-kept homes and we were used to keeping clean, so I don't know what they were expecting. Perhaps they thought all the evacuees would be from the slums and crawling with lice or something! But we were very comfortable, as far as the house was concerned.'

'And how did the Marlowes treat you? Did you feel that you were part of their family?'

'Absolutely not! They were wealthy people, and I suppose they'd brought their children up the way aristocrats do. They were very strict

with us. Children stayed with the servants until they were old enough –
civilized enough, maybe – to be with them, and that's how they treated
us. We were to be seen and not heard from – and preferably not seen,
either! They really didn't want to know anything about us or about
our well-being. At least, that's how we felt. We were never allowed to
sit in their rooms with them to eat. We had to sit in the kitchen with
the cook and the two Swiss maids and whatever other servants were
working there on any given day – gardeners and handymen, and so on.
Those maids, by the way, went back to Switzerland because of the war.
Switzerland was neutral and I think they were ordered home by the
Home Office.'

'*Were you ever invited into their part of the house?*'

'Only very rarely. But on the day after we arrived – we'd only been
there one day – they brought us into their big living room with its
floor-to-ceiling windows, magnificent curtains and carpets, antique
furniture, and works of art on the walls – we were not usually allowed
to go in there, we were told – and they sat us down in front of the
fireplace on deep, upholstered armchairs to listen to the wireless.
We heard Neville Chamberlain, who was the Prime Minister at
that time, announce that England was at war with Germany, that
the ultimatum sent to Adolf Hitler about moving the troops out of
Poland was ignored, so we were automatically at war. Soon after that
announcement, an air raid siren went off. We had no idea what was
going on, but the lady of the house very calmly showed us how to
put our gas masks on, and we were to sit in the living room with our
gas masks on until the all-clear sounded and we were allowed to take
the gas masks off. Remember, it was September, it was hot, and it
was very uncomfortable with those rubbery-smelling masks over our
noses and mouths! And it was thirty minutes before the all clear! It
seemed a whole lot longer.'

'*How long did you all stay with this family?*'

'Well, we came on 2 September and I left the day before Christmas.
My girl friend left before that. I can't remember exactly, but I think
she was there about six weeks. She was very unhappy and homesick,
and she was crying a lot of the time, so she finally asked her parents to
come and take her back to London. I stuck it out until the time the
school broke for the holidays. I said to my sister, "we're going home to
London, because I'll be fourteen and I'm going out to work and earn a

living. And I'm not leaving you here with the Marlowes on your own."
So I wrote to my mother and asked her to come down and pick us up.
That's how we left.'

*'You haven't mentioned much about school. What happened to your education
while you were away?'*

'Education was shot to hell!' She broke into laughter at her own
outspokenness. 'When we arrived at Boxmore, my sister and I were
advised that we would be told when we could go to school. So, for two
weeks we had a holiday. There wasn't a lot for us to do. We went for long
walks in the countryside and I read stories to my little sister. We even
helped the cook in the kitchen on some days. Then, arrangements were
made for my sister to go to the village school. It was very convenient
for her. It was just at the bottom of the lane, and she was able to go
straight away because of her age. Older girls had to go to an elementary
school and the only one available was in Hemel Hempstead. So, after
two weeks of waiting, they informed us that we would be taken to the
school. We were to meet at Boxmore station and we would be taken
to school on a bus. We were taken to West Hertfordshire Elementary,
which was a very beautiful, modern building. We went every day for
two weeks but the classes were chaotic. There were far too many of
us, combined with the Hemel Hempstead children. The rooms were
just packed. After that, we were told "Don't report to that school next
week!" In other words, they didn't want us London evacuees coming to
their new school, and there was nothing we could do about it because
they weren't part of the London school system. They could tell us if
they wanted us or not. It was their school.

We didn't go to school at all for about three weeks after that and
we finally ended up forming classes with our own teachers in a local
church hall in Hemel Hempstead. The vicar of the church took pity
on us and allocated us two of his Sunday school rooms to hold classes
in – and we did the best we could with what we had. We had three
teachers. There were five classes in one room. We just took the basics:
reading, writing, and arithmetic. We couldn't do anything else. That's all
we could do.' She shrugged, conveying the limitations of a 'one-room'
school.

Education was only one deprivation endured by Irene in these three
months away from home. She missed the comfort of a mother to speak
with about womanly things, the lady of the house being much too
distant, emotionally, for girlish confidences. 'I wouldn't have dreamed
of talking to her about such things.'

Irene had started her periods in June of 1939, before leaving London in September. Once away, she grew more and more worried and embarrassed. She watched every month but had no period in September, or October. In October, she developed a terrible rash. There was an epidemic of impetigo among the children and Mrs Marlowe thought Irene had contracted it. She rushed her to the doctor – 'She was absolutely hysterical,' Irene said. 'She thought I was dirty, or something.' The doctor asked Mrs Marlowe to wait outside while Irene was examined. He asked the girl her age and quickly realised that her rash was related to changes in her hormonal balance. 'The doctor told Mrs Marlowe that it was caused by "growing up" and he prescribed calamine lotion to treat the spots,' Irene said.

Mrs Marlowe drove Irene to the chemist's but then went off in the car to do some shopping, leaving the girl to walk home alone. Unfortunately, Irene dropped the bottle on the way and broke it, splashing lotion everywhere. She burst into tears and was still crying when she arrived at the house, feeling utterly humiliated. Irregular periods are not unusual at the onset of menses, but the girl did not have her mother to tell her these things and she was embarrassed to turn to strangers.

Notable too is that elementary school children were no longer considered 'children' the moment they turned fourteen, the school leaving age. Irene took it for granted then, and still, even so many decades later, that she had 'aged out' of the school system and that she must leave the area and return to London, a danger zone. The government authorities would no longer take responsibility for her safety.

Phyllis's Story

Phyllis, Irene's little sister, was seven years old when she left her Newington Green school for Boxmore, near Hemel Hempstead, in Hertfordshire.

'I honestly don't remember anything about getting there, going on the bus, or the train. Nothing. I know I was with my sister, and I know I held onto her hand as tightly as I could, but I don't remember anything else much, not even how we found our way to our billet. I was only seven, after all.'

'*Do you remember anything about the place you went to and the way you were treated?*' I asked.

'Oh, it was a very beautiful home, I do remember that, and they had a tennis court, which impressed me very much. And they had maids and a cook. I remember the man of the house. He was very dark-skinned, swarthy, even, and their name was Marlowe, I think. He was a Sephardic Jew but I think his wife was not. More likely Ashkenazi, but she didn't seem to want to acknowledge her Jewishness at all. He was an importer/exporter in the city – at least, that's what I understand now.

They were both highly intelligent, educated people and they spoke very nicely. They were like gentry, I guess you'd call them. It was a beautiful place and I think we had a nice bedroom but it's all rather vague. I don't remember too much about living there.'

'*Do you recall having meals with the Marlowes, or spending any time with them?*'

'No. Their part of the house was off limits to us. That was made clear from the first day. We had our meals with the cook and the maids in the kitchen. We didn't really have much contact with the people who owned the house. The only time we sat with them was when we were called in to listen to Neville Chamberlain on the wireless telling us that we were at war with Germany. I really didn't understand much of that.'

'*How long did you stay in the Marlowe's house?*'

'Well, we got there at the beginning of September and I think we left in December. My sister was going to be fourteen on 5 December, and at that time she was going to leave school and go to work. I assume that my mother came to fetch us and we went home, at least for a while but that part is all a bit dim in my mind.

The funny thing was that we went back to Boxmore, just my mother and me, and we stayed in a lady's house in the same village, like lodgers.

My sister must have stayed with my grandparents in London, because she was working by then. I remember the lady we were with, the landlady, as nice and chubby and very warm and motherly. That was maybe for a couple of months and then my mother decided to go back to London because it was what they called 'the phoney war' and nothing was happening, no bombing or anything. There didn't seem to be any reason to stay away when we could be in our own home.'

'How did you get on in London when you went back?'

'Well, we continued to live our lives. I had some schooling, but there were no formal schools open in the area, so I remember I had a couple of months of going to different ladies' houses for schooling. There were like six children and the lady would teach us how to read and write. I don't know if they were trained teachers or not; they may just have been neighbourhood ladies. Schooling was terribly disrupted. And then my mother found out there was a school in Mildmay Road called St Jude's that was open and they were giving lessons. So I went to St Jude's until later in that year, 1940. Then, I don't know why, my mother decided to evacuate me again. I don't remember any bombing or any air raids. I think maybe they were starting. Anyway, she decided I had to go out of London. I'm sure she thought she was doing the best thing for me.'

'Where did you go this time?'

'Well, I do remember a bit about going away the second time. We went to Wales. South Wales. Monmouthshire, which I understand is now called Gwent. It was like the first evacuation all over again. A whole crowd of children in Islington and Stoke Newington were gathered up and labelled, with our suitcases and our gas masks. My mother didn't come with me and I don't remember her even coming to see me off. It was only children and some teachers and some Women's Voluntary Services people. I was eight by that time. We went by train from Paddington, I think, to Wales, and then on a bus.'

'Do you remember how you were assigned a place to stay?'

'Yes, that part is quite clear. I remember going up a street on the bus, which I think was the central avenue of the village of Oakdale. There was a man on the bus – I don't know who he was but he may have been a teacher – and he would say 'Okay, you get off here and go with those people, and you get of here and go with those people'. And that's how they did it!'

'What happened when you arrived at the house with the people who took you in?'

'Well, my mother had always said, "no matter where you go, no matter what happens to you, you must always remember that you are a Jewish child". So, I came into the house and they sat me down in the middle of the room (she laughs as she tells the story) and all the neighbours came in to look at me. And I told them my name and then I said "and I'm Jewish!" And they all stared and one lady said, "What do you mean? What's that? (She laughs, again). And I said, 'Well, that's my religion. My faith." And I tried to explain and, well, I was eight years old. What did I know! I didn't know how to explain this. And I – they were church-going people, where I was billeted. They had read the bible from cover to cover. They knew about Jews. They knew about the Old Testament. So they must have known what "Jewish" meant, but it didn't seem to make any impression on them. It could be that they were just having a bit of harmless fun with me.' She paused as though considering this possibility for the first time. She smiled and continued, 'I don't think they even cared what my religion was. And that was it. That was my introduction to my new home.

The people were John and Annie Turner and one of the first things they said to me after this was "You must write to your mother and tell her where you are…" They were sensitive to how my mother must be feeling. I told them that I didn't have a father, that he had died the year before, so I think they were particularly concerned about my widowed mother. They were lovely, caring people; they would have been in their forties, I should think. They had two children, a daughter of twelve – who resented me a little bit, I think, and an older child, a son, who was already at the Air Force Academy. I was a bit of a klutz at that time and I remember spilling some tea and feeling so mortified that I burst into tears, but they soon made me feel that it didn't matter. They were such kind people.'

'What was the Turner's religion, and did they expect you to go to church?'

'Well, they went to chapel. They were devout Presbyterian chapel people and I said that, you know, I didn't go to chapel. So in the beginning, and for quite a long time, somebody would stay in the house with me when they went to chapel. For instance, somebody would go to the evening service, somebody would go to the morning service. And whoever didn't go to the service would stay at home with me.

So, I didn't think much about it but I think they were upset. It seemed that I was preventing them from enjoying going to chapel together, and this was very important to them, the togetherness, So, they let it slide for about two or three months.

Eventually, my family started coming to see me: my mother, my grandparents, my sister. My aunt and uncle came, too. And they got into a serious conversation with the Turners.

They asked them that if, God forbid, they all got killed in the war, would these people take care of me and help me grow into, you know, adulthood. And the Turners said they would – but they would like me to join in with their chapel-going. My family said that would be fine. I wonder, sometimes, if it really was fine with them, and I wished I'd talked about it with them later. They weren't really devout Jews, my family, but they were Jewish and it must have gone against their grain a bit for them to agree to my being brought up as a Christian – should the worst happen.'

'*I assume they were wonderful people for your family to have asked them to do this for you – and to have agreed to do as the Turners requested.*'

'Well, the Turners liked me and they wanted me to assimilate into their lives and to be part of their lives, and since I was in their house and I enjoyed being in their house, then I should do whatever they did. So they gradually started taking me to chapel.'

'*How did you like that?*'

She smiled, clearly happy to be recounting these memories. 'As it happens, I used to sing. I loved the hymns and I would join in the choir, I really enjoyed all of it. I mean, it wasn't a chore; it was a very enjoyable experience. I enjoyed Sunday school. I enjoyed learning the psalms and verses, and I used to have wonderful discussions with the teachers about all the different aspects of the Bible and it was never a chore. It was a joy, really.'

She paused, and to my surprise, she began to sing, her voice low and sweet:

For the beauty of the earth,
For the beauty of the skies,
For the love which from our birth,
Over and around us lies:
Father unto thee we raise
This our sacrifice of praise.

For the beauty of each hour,
Of the day and of the night,
Hill and vale, and tree and flower,
Sun and moon and stars of light…

'But I always remembered I was Jewish' she added. 'And that never changed.'

We sat quietly for several moments, before I continued my questioning:

'You were evidently treated very well by the Turners.'

'They couldn't have been nicer or kinder to me if they'd been my own parents. The lady was a wonderful cook. You see, they didn't have modern stoves to cook on. They did everything on the fire. And they had an oven with the fire on all the year round. That was because there was a water boiler at the back of the fireplace for hot water. And they had a big tub in the kitchen with a lid over it. I'll never forget those bath nights, filling the tub with water heated in the boiler. At home, we had a proper bathroom, but, here, the tub was in the kitchen. Mrs Turner was also a marvellous washer. She would make the clothes crisp and white and gorgeous, and we'd hang them on the line and they would smell so sweet. when we brought them back into the house. And she made dresses for me. She was always very, very nice. Her hands… she had golden hands.'

'Were you aware of what was happening to your family while you were in Wales?'

'Well, yes. We had been bombed out, both my mother's and my grandparents' flats. The roofs had been destroyed by incendiary bombs and most of the windows were blown out. I think they had been living in the air raid shelter a lot of the time and it was a terribly harrowing experience for everybody. They were in a public shelter, I think, surrounded by strangers, and they didn't like it one bit. They spoke sometimes of friends who had an Anderson shelter in their garden. It was a kind of underground room – or partly underground room – made of corrugated metal, and people made them quite comfortable with proper bunks to sleep on. Not ideal, but better than the public shelters. I think one of the reasons my family came down to see me quite frequently was because it gave them some respite from the bombing. It was the bombing, of course, and the real possibility that they might be killed, that led to their asking the Turners if they would take care of me until I could take care of myself. Thank God, that wasn't necessary.'

'*When did you return to London?*'

'I stayed with the people through 1941, '42, and '43. I went back to London in 1944 I think, and I stayed in London until the doodlebugs started and then I went back to the Turners again for another few months – six months, I think. They welcomed me back just as if I'd been their child. I recall being there in 1945. The war was over and I remember we had big parties. But I was only visiting, then, I wasn't there on a permanent basis. I was going back to London. Later, I always went back to visit and I kept in touch with them for years. Such kind people!'

Three

Bill Reed's Story

My interview with Bill was in his spacious and elegantly furnished house in a charming residential neighbourhood. He had clearly been successful in life, in ways that gave him a sense of achievement and status. A businessman, he was self-assured and spoke in glowing terms of his relatively brief stay in the country as an evacuee, and of the positive influence his hosts there had had upon him. For the most part, he spoke with a general south of England accent; every now and then, a cockney syllable or two would slip into his speech, a remnant of his earlier life. His wife, Joyce, whom I also interviewed, remained proudly, defiantly, and charmingly cockney, completely comfortable with who she was, where she had come from, and where she had arrived.

'I was thirteen and a few months when I was evacuated,' Bill began. 'Almost fourteen years old. We lived in Chiswick at the time, in Devonshire Road, which is not too far from Kew Gardens. I went with my school to Hemel Hempstead. Actually it was a small town called Little Gadderson, which was between Hemel Hempstead and Berkhampstead. We walked, a long line of us, from school to the railway station, carrying our luggage and our gas masks. We had been practicing wiv our gas masks for a couple of days, putting them on and making sure they were airtight. I remember hoping we would never had to use them for real, because they were suffocating!'

'The train took us to Hemel Hempstead, and when we got there, we were all loaded into a coach or a bus and we drove a mile or two, I guess, out of the town and into a more rural area. Then the bus stopped and we all piled out. There was a crowd of people waiting there, and they would select the children they wanted to take, whoever they liked the look of, I suppose. And then the bus, with us aboard again, would go down a hundred yards or so. We would pile off the bus again and walk as a group, and people would come out of their houses, or the teachers knocked on the doors to let people know we were there. And, again, they would select the ones they thought they would like. We did this several times, on and off the bus. Early on, it seemed that everybody wanted the young ladies and the guys and the boys were left to the last. That seemed to be the pattern as it went along. I don't know if they thought the girls might be better at doing housework, or more well-behaved, perhaps. When it came to my turn to be selected, I was very fortunate. I know now that I was very fortunate. They selected two boys. One of them was a person I knew quite well. I didn't go to school with him but he lived a few houses from us. Jackie Gilbert was his name. We were picked by the James people, who owned the local butcher shop. Along with the husband and wife, there were three daughters, all very friendly, and we were treated exceptionally well, probably a lot better than I had been treated at home. The treatment I got and the food I got, I didn't know existed.'

'So you would say yours was a happy experience and that you had a really good time?'

'Yes. I had a very good experience and a very good time, doing things that were a heck of a lot different from anything I had ever done before. Living in the country was a whole new and wonderful experience for me. As I said, we stayed wiv the local butcher and we used to go out early in the morning to set the traps to try to catch rabbits – things like that. They used to hunt pheasants, as well. I didn't get involved in that because it needed guns, and obviously we boys were not ready for guns. But we had a good time setting traps where the rabbits would run, and we were taught how to do that properly. I was also taught how to skin a rabbit. It was a young age to be able to do that well.'

'I can't imagine how you would start a task like that – and you from Chiswick, where rabbits come already skinned on a slab in the butcher's shop!'

'Yes, people do get a bit freaked out when I tell them about it. And, as they say, there's more than one way to skin a rabbit!' He laughed. 'I was taught well.' He paused, as if wondering if he should elaborate, and then continued. 'We made a cut between the thighs first, and pulled the skin off the legs, then pulled the skin down all the way to the front legs and right off. Finally, we removed the innards. Some people remove the innards first…' He paused, and grinned at me. 'This is probably more information than you need, right?'

'Thank you. As much as I want to know!' We both laughed. *'Still it sounds as though rabbit provided some of the good food you ate while you were with the James family.'*

'Oh yes, all the food was quite good – including rabbit pie. It didn't seem we were on rations at all. One thing I did notice in the morning that was a surprise to me at that time, I came down that first day to breakfast and they had this enormous big pot on the stove and the aroma was different from anything I'd smelled before. I remember the people telling me that we were going to have porridge oats for breakfast and I said "I don't like porridge oats" just because, of course, I had never had them. At least I couldn't recall ever having them. But there was this enormous pot, and they served the oats, and I didn't know whether to eat them or not. But I was pretty darned hungry – that good fresh country air – and I found I really enjoyed them.'

'So you were well fed and you enjoyed the hunting and so on. What about other activities besides setting traps and skinning rabbits?'

'Oh, I joined in all kinds of different activities. I played football and cricket wiv the local people. As a matter of fact, we used to have a lot of tournament type of things. There was a local team, local people, who played against us. They always seemed as though they played better than we did, but we were much rougher and tougher than they were, so we always won! I used to play cricket in the summer when we first went there, and later, we played soccer.'

'You mentioned that it was there that you learned to play golf and it was at that time that you developed your love of golf.'

'One thing that always comes to my mind is that we were pretty darn close to where Henry Cotton used to play golf down there. There was a course in the area and I was fortunate to be wiv people who belonged to this country club. They used to take me along sometimes and I learned how to play – or, at least, I tried to learn how to play. As you can imagine, I became really enthusiastic about golf and played it whenever I could – but that was a beautiful golf course there. I couldn't get enough of it.'

'How long were you away?'

'The duration I was away I can't really remember, I think it's because the time went so fast. I was so involved in everything I did there, but

I believe it was about six or eight months. I did have a problem because of that, because of my schooling. It was a little different…'

'I'm not sure I understand what you mean. But I was going to ask you about how your schooling was affected.'

'I guess I was fortunate enough to pass the 'O Levels' or whatever they were called at that time. I think that's what they were, I've forgotten. It may have just been the exam for the High School. Anyway, I went to Chiswick Central School at home, so I had passed some exam or other. It was a different school from the one Jackie Gilbert, the boy who was with me at the James', went to, but in Little Gadderson, we all went to the same school, Jackie and me and the three young ladies who were in the house – the James' daughters. The education was definitely not as good as I had been getting in Chiswick, mainly because we had just one teacher who kind of taught everything. We didn't get into the kinds of studies quite as much as we would have done at home. It seemed to be pretty basic, just the three R's. I got the feeling that was why my parents took me home. I'm pretty sure there were all kinds of gaps in my knowledge after that time because we didn't have any really good schooling for quite a while.'

'How did you get on when you got back to London? Were you involved in the bombing at all?'

'When we got back to London, the Blitz was just beginning. Being a kid, it didn't bother me too much one way or another. I don't remember being scared, but I was amazed to find the areas where I used to play now had air raid shelters built under them. Right under the playground. You'd have to go down a few steps to get into them. The bombing got really heavy, not long after I got home, and we were supposed to stay down the shelters every night. I vividly remember that one night I was in the shelter having a discussion with a very good friend of mine called Dido Smith. I don't know how we got onto the topic, but we were talking about the subject of life. And I mentioned to him, "Well, anybody could get killed. It's a matter of fate. You're either fated to be killed, or you're not. You don't have a heck of a lot of choice about it." And that very night, his brother and his father – he didn't have a mother – his brother and his father stayed in their house and a bomb hit the house – a direct hit – and killed them both. It's always stayed in my mind. Why should I have said a thing like that at that particular time to a very good friend of mine? I never saw him again after that…'

He paused, clearly moved by this particular reminiscence, before continuing. 'I do think fate, or luck, or chance, or whatever you want to call it, plays a larger part in our lives than we like to think. Yes, you have to work hard if you want to get on; you have to have a goal. But it was fate that landed me with the James people. I could have been picked by anyone, couldn't I, and had a quite different story to tell?'

'Yours was one of the happier experiences of the evacuation that I have heard about, and it is clear that it left some lasting impressions on you, especially with your golf...'

'Yes, my evacuation experience did a couple of things for me, I think. I learned, basically, how to be competitive, which I didn't know how to be in London. Everybody there did things basically the way everybody else did them, and people around me didn't seem to have any aims or goals. They just sort of lived day to day, taking what came. But living and working with a family who were business people and had a goal in life of getting on – that was different. They taught me how to be competitive, they taught me how to fend for myself, which I wouldn't have known how to do before, such as hunting for rabbits, and those kind of things. Also, there was the golf. I learned how to play golf and that has affected me a lot. I had always played a lot of sports growing up but whatever I played I always came back to playing golf. And now, I still have the challenge of the game, which I play as often as I can – but not as often as I would like, perhaps. So I guess the introduction to golf at that impressionable time in my life has left two things with me: one, how to play the game – I like it so much – and, two, how to be competitive.'

Four

Joyce Reed's Story

Joyce, seated in an armchair nearby, listened intently as Bill, her husband, told me about his experiences as an evacuee with the James family. When he spoke of his friend's loss of father and brother in London's Blitz, though, she stirred uneasily, clearly wanting to say something, but not wanting to impinge on Bill's reminiscences. I wondered if she had heard his stories before or whether evacuees, like soldiers who have seen action on the battlefield, generally keep their more painful experiences locked away, even from their wives. Certainly, all the people I interviewed were eager to talk to me in great detail, with an outpouring of words that perhaps they had been holding inside for a long time.

When it was Joan's turn to answer my questions, she exchanged seats with Bill and breathed deeply, as though preparing to release a store of memories. A gentle, sweet-voiced woman, she began hesitantly, with single-word answers to my questions, but she gradually relaxed and the words – and much laughter – flowed freely.

'I was twelve, almost thirteen when I was evacuated. It seemed inevitable that there was going to be a war when we were issued with gas masks, and when they started taking the railings away round the houses – to melt down for ammunition, we were told. My family lived in Acton Green in London and I went away with my school, Beaumont Park School. We waved goodbye to our parents and walked to the school with those gas masks and a few belongings. We climbed on a double-decker bus to the railway station and then we boarded a train. Our destination was Dorchester, in Dorset, although we didn't know where we were going at the time.'

'What happened when you got to Dorchester?'

'Well, we came off the train and we all had to line up in twos. The houses were kind of right there by the station and, immediately, the children were going straight into these houses. We'd go down one street and then onto another street, with the teachers knocking on doors as we walked. We'd go two children here, one there, three there, and so on. That's how they did it. We didn't have any idea what the people were like or anything. I was hoping that my friend and I would be billeted together, but she went to the house next door.'

'You said earlier that you were in more than one billet. What can you remember about the first people who took you in?'

'Well, I went into a very nice home at first, an affluent home. They were high-class people – at least, they seemed to think they were. The couple had two daughters, one at boarding school and one at home, a bit younger than me. He was a banker, and I was kind of shy with them. I wasn't used to people like that. They had a living-in maid and she agreed to sleep out because of me, and I slept in the maid's room. The maid came every day and cooked and cleaned, but I had to do my own laundry, make my bed, and mop my room every day. Then the maid decided she wanted to go and serve in the armed forces. The lady couldn't manage without her so then I had to go somewhere else. I was there for about two or two and a half months, I think.'

'The lady of the house was a bit on the snobby side – and me being a cockney an' all. As soon as I got into the house, she asked me if I would like to take a bath. That was the very first thing she wanted me to do before we went down to supper. And I told her I didn't think I could take a bath because I was not well. Actually, I was having my period and I was worried about what I should say. I had asked my mother before I left and she told me what to say. The lady seemed to understand without me having to spell it out. She said I could just have a wash down, then. As I said, I had the little boxroom, which was the maid's room, and there was a china bowl and jug to use for washing. They had a bathroom, but she expected me to use the bowl and jug. Actually, there was another room belonging to the daughter who was away at school. It had a sink in it. I'd never seen a bedroom with a sink in it. That room was left empty, except when the daughter came home for holidays. After I washed myself and tidied my hair, I went down to supper.'

'As young as I was, I knew they thought that I was not as high-class as what they were and I know – she actually told me this – that she thought that all Londoners lived on fish and chips. And so, when we sat down to eat it was rather formal, with several sets of knives and forks lined up, and they had napkins. Well, I honestly had never used a napkin before, and they were cloth napkins, as well. In napkin holders. I just watched everyone else and saw how they picked up their napkins.'

'They'd already picked up their knives and forks, and I hadn't, so I took a guess on which ones to choose. And I was wrong!' She laughed, remembering the inexperienced child she had been. 'And they corrected me. I really think they was waiting for me to do something wrong, that they sort of expected me to. They was just all lookin' at me, sort of studyin' me. So of course I made a mistake. I think anybody would have made a mistake if they were nervous and, after all, I wasn't used to that formal way of eating, with two or three sets of knives and forks lined up.' She grinned as she looked around her handsomely furnished living room, towards the dining room that could be seen through the glass double doors. In the decades since the evacuation, she had obviously moved up the social ladder.

In the course of our time together, I learned that she and Bill were building a grand new house overlooking the local country club. Clearly, she had grown used to cloth napkins and no longer needed to be shown how to use them, nor did she need instruction about which set of cutlery to pick up for which course.

'We were rationed in that house, right off the bat, even before rationing really began. At teatime, we'd have bread and the lady would say, "Do you want butter or jam with that" and she'd put a tiny ring of one or the other on your plate. I hate to talk about her like this, but she had cupboards full of jam that she had made from blackberries and other fruit that she had picked. And at the beginning of the war, she still had mountains of sugar. I think she must have had it there for years. But she rationed us because Cynthia, her daughter at boarding school, wrote that they had begun to ration them there. We'd hardly been supplied with our ration books. One good thing, though, that she did for me – we learned to take our tea without sugar. So when I got home, I wondered what was wrong with my tea. I didn't like it because I preferred tea without sugar. Still do. I do recall that I wasn't allowed to say "okay" in that house. It seems unimportant now, but I'll remember it always, and how strict she was about it, the lady of the house. I think she really resented the fact that she had to take in an evacuee. I believe she had the option of taking a soldier or an evacuee. That was their choice, and they really didn't want to do either. People are people, I guess.'

'*You told me earlier about a swimsuit the lady lent you. I'd like to hear more about that.*' Joyce smiled, and then burst into laughter.

'It seems funny now, but it wasn't so funny then. In fact, I was mortified. At school, they told us they were going to take us to the coast, to Weymouth. I was so excited because I loved to swim. It was my favourite sport, that was. "Oh, I don't have a swimsuit" I told the lady of the house, "I left it at home." "Don't worry about that," the lady said, and she took me up into the attic, opened this trunk and dug out this swimsuit. I nearly had a fit when I saw it! It must have dated back to the 1920s. Even though I was young, I could see that. Kind of black at the bottom and striped at the top? Of course, I was very self-conscious at that age because of my developing figure, and my own costumes were those elastic type ones, which I loved because they were kind of bumpy all over and hid your own bumps. This one was so old fashioned! I went into the water – and when I came out, I had to cover myself with my arms because the thing clung to me. I was soooo... I don't know what word to use to describe what it did to me. That evening, when I got back to the house, I wrote to my mother and I had to draw a diagram of the suit to let her really see, to prove what it was like. I was such a traumatic thing...' Again, her peals of laughter filled the room.

'*You were at the first place about two or three months, you said. What kind of place did you go to after that?*'

'Well, I went to the complete opposite. It was funny, really, because it was out of the frying pan and into the fire. At the first house, I had to be home at a certain time, but with these other people, they didn't care what time I came home. And I never had a bath, there. There was no bathroom. It was a kind of "do as you like" place. My mother was not at all happy when she came and visited me. So I guess I was there only about a month. In the first house, I had my own bedroom, but in this house there were six of us: the woman of the house and her daughter, and two of us evacuees. We two girls slept in a bed together and the older lady and her daughter slept together, the four of us in one room. And the husband slept in another room with a son.'

'*What did your mother say when she visited and saw how you were living?*'

'Well, she wanted to take me home but she couldn't do that straight away. She had to make some arrangements before I went home.

The funny part about it was that I didn't realise how grubby I was until my mother came to visit, and I remember her washing my neck and washing my neck. And the other evacuee – we came from the same area and we'd known each other before – her mother also came, and she was doing exactly the same with her daughter – washing her neck and washing her neck. That was funny!'

'*How did you feel about going home?*'

'Glad! I was glad about going home. I'd wanted to go home when I was in the first place because I really didn't like it there. I really wanted to be able to say "okay".' She smiled. 'And all those things that happened there made me feel uncomfortable, small somehow, as though I was less than what they were. I was homesick, too, but my mother thought I was in a good place and that I should stay there as long as they'd have me.'

'*What happened when you went home?*'

'Well, we went back to school. We had all these substitute teachers. We'd never experienced that kind of teacher before. The teachers we'd had prior to that were very, very strict. These others weren't like teachers to us, so we just told them what to do, 'cos they didn't seem to know. I left school when I was fourteen. I think you could leave on your actual birthday, so I did just that. I left on my birthday. There was an air raid on at the same time as I left school.'

'*It sounds as though you got back to London in time for the Blitz.*'

'Yes. The Blitz started just as I left school. I had two girl friends that I went to school with. One I'd known since I was six or seven, and she was killed with a – I don't know how many ton bomb it was but it was a bomb that was so bad that they never found their bodies, 'cos they lived right where the crater was, my friend and her brother and her mother. So they had the funeral service right there on the crater.

Then I had another girl friend – I think it was a year or a couple of years later – killed with a buzz bomb. She lived right across the street from where my other friend was killed. And I lived a few yards further down. We had to get out of our house. It was condemned. Lucky for us, though, we was spared.'

'*So your house was also bombed?*'

'Yes. There was a railway at the bottom of our garden. The railway was a temptation to the German bombers 'cos it was main line. Troops and ammunition travelled on it. Even German prisoners of war went across, and the Red Cross wounded soldiers. They all went along that line. So the German tried to bomb the railway, but they missed it and got the houses instead. The whole thing seems unreal when I look back on it. I don't think the seriousness of it strikes you when you're a kid. And you put it out of your mind quicker. I remember being worried that my mother seemed so nervous all the time.'

We sat quietly for a few moments as Joyce relived the horrors she had seen, and realised their full extent. I changed the subject. '*I would really like to know more about the schooling you had, perhaps in a little more detail.*'

'Well, when we arrived in Dorchester, it took a while for the teachers and everybody to get organized for school. They finally found us a hall and we went there for a few hours most days. I'm not sure how long it was in the beginning. We just sat around with the teachers in groups on little chairs and that was it. We didn't have a desk or anything. And that went on for a while and it wasn't very successful. Finally, they was able to persuade the schools in the country there to share their schools with us. We went in the afternoons and the local children went in the mornings. And that was the schooling! And when I got back to London, that was the end. My schooling just went to pot! It was over. It was over, really, from the time I got on that bus at the school on the way to being evacuated.'

'Still, I think there's more to education than going to school. My formal education kind of finished, but Dorchester happened to be a very historic town. It dates all the way back to the Iron Age. And it was an old Roman town. The Romans built a town there in the year [AD] 43. There were ancient walls, and an amphitheatre, and I was interested in all that stuff and started to learn about it. It was much more than reading and writing and arithmetic, it was the study of the old Roman ruins. Thomas Hardy lived there, too, and Casterbridge in The Mayor of Casterbridge was really Dorchester, so I had plenty of interesting stuff to learn about there. I could go on and on about that stuff… but I won't!' She laughed. 'Let me make us a cup of tea, instead!'

Five

My Story, Part Two

Britain was at war with Germany but no shots were fired, no bombs came screaming from the skies, no sirens sounded to summon the people to shelter. The Germans were engaged in the Polish campaign and had no bases to launch an attack of fighters and bombers. So month followed month and little changed but the seasons.

Out in his well-ordered workshop at the end of the garden, Uncle Bert built sturdy wooden frames to fit every window in the house and carefully stretched dark, opaque leather-cloth over them so that the cloth lay smooth, the corners neatly mitred. I marvelled at the way he worked, surely, methodically, choosing from the neatly arranged tools the precise instrument for each purpose. Nails and screws of graded sizes were housed in small, well-made drawers, hammers hung on the wall next to saws and pliers and wire-cutters and wrenches and chisels, so that the whole formed a picture of gleaming metal and wood, a work of art. Opposite hung another composition of gardening implements: forks and spades and shears and hoes and rakes, all maintained in perfect order, every trace of mud lovingly wiped away after each use. Bert Brown's shed was his haven, his release after long days at the foundry, his retreat from a house full of females, the only place in the world he had total autonomy. Aunty Doll and Colleen and Merle were allowed into the shed, and now me too, but only if we were very quiet and spoke only at the rare times we were addressed.

I liked the smell of the shed, a combination of wood-shavings and turpentine and other aromatic oils. I sat silently on one of the work benches and watched Uncle Bert as he folded the heavy fabric around one of the frames and tacked it tidily into place with small nails plucked from several he held firmly between his lips.

'I wonder how my Daddy is blacking out the windows at home,' I pondered, forgetting for a moment to keep silent.

I had once seen my Dad bang some nails into a wall for use as coat hangers, but he bought the nails especially for the purpose, and borrowed the hammer from a neighbour. 'He says he can fix anything with a nail file and common sense,' I added, hoping it didn't sound as if my Dad was boasting.

'Oh aye.' Uncle Bert removed the nails from his mouth to acknowledge my remarks, and then continued his careful pinning and hammering. I could see that, even for my clever Daddy, a nail file might not serve this task.

Each evening before tea – the 'high tea' of cold sliced meats and salad and beetroots in vinegar, or meat pie and vegetables from the garden – we children fitted the blackouts to the insides of the windows and dashed outside, giggling and racing each other, to make sure no light showed through. In the morning, before the rest of the household was awake, Uncle Bert took the blackouts down and stowed them behind the upright piano in the little-used front parlour. This putting up and taking down of the blackouts became a ritual, a routine if empty exercise, for no enemy hovered over the house, seeking chinks in our armour.

I soon became accustomed to the regular cycle of domestic events in the Brown household. At the weekends, Uncle Bert tended his garden, digging, weeding, mulching, planting, as the seasons dictated. The small garden at the front of the sturdy, brick bungalow remained largely ornamental, with shrubs planted along the sides of the dwelling slowly growing dense and high enough to provide a measure of privacy from the identical bungalows crowding alongside. In the back garden, divided by a straight, narrow concrete path placed precisely down the centre, Uncle Bert planted vegetables for the table. Cabbages especially flourished, in spite of the green caterpillars that shared them with the family. Sometimes the path was so thick with the insects as they concertina'd from one side of the garden to the other, that I walked in the moist earth rather than risk squashing bright green stains into the cement.

Monday was washing day. No matter what the weather, immediately after breakfast, Aunty Doll lit the gas copper in the scullery, scrubbed load after load of linens on a washboard in hot sudsy water in the big kitchen sink, and then put them to boil in the copper. She opened the outside door so the steam could escape and, although all the other doors were firmly closed, the smell of boiling cloth permeated every room in the house.

'Isn't that hard work for you?' I asked, watching Aunty Doll straining to lift the wet clothes out of the boiling water with wooden tongs, wring them through rollers, and heave them into cold rinsing water in the sink. She would then wring the clothes again, and hang them on several rope lines across the back garden. On wet days, she draped the clothes over the Dutch airer suspended from the scullery ceiling.

'The things look so heavy…'

'Doosn't your moother do the wash this way, then?'

'No, 'cos we don't have a copper at home. My Mum goes to the bag-wash.'

'The bag-wash? What's that, then?'

I hesitated, not sure if I could explain. 'Well, the dirty things are all tied together in a bundle, and my Mum takes them to the laundry. They only wash them there and Mummy has to bring them home to dry them.' I paused, thinking about how my mother dragged the bundle home, a much heavier bundle, now that it was wet, breathing hard as she climbed the wooden stairs. She hung the damp, wrinkled pieces over the banister railing, the railing that looked over the stairs that led, first, to the bathroom, then to the Schmidt's flat and, then, to the street. Hung several layers deep, the clothes took a long time to dry and they exuded a mustiness quite unlike the sweet, fresh-air smell of Aunty Doll's sheets and towels and pillow cases.

While Uncle Bert worked in his garden, Aunty Doll and we girls went for long walks or bicycle rides into the open country that began at the end of their road. A walk through the churchyard on the corner brought us to farmlands crossed by little-travelled roads, safe for family excursions. Colleen showed me how to ride the old machine Uncle Bert rode to work every morning.

'It's a bit foony, cocking your leg over like that to mount, boot once you're on it, it'll be all right, you'll see.'

'Ow! Don't let me fall, Colleen!' I pretended to be frightened, sensing it was expected, but I found my balance in moments, as though I'd been born to bicycle, and I was soon speeding along the roads, loving the way my hair streamed out behind me, gently tugged back by the breeze I generated. I had dreamed of having a bicycle ever since I could remember. I was in kid heaven!

Sheep and cows grazed in the fields, and berries grew along the hedgerows. In late September and early October, we girls picked baskets of blackberries and Aunty Doll potted jam and jelly and baked pies that were left to cool on the wide, tiled shelves of the larder.

As the weather turned colder, Aunty Doll began her sewing for us children. She took the bus into Peterborough to buy cloth from 'the Jew boys,' she said, purely descriptively. Small shops in Paston also sold fabric but prices were better in Peterborough.

Although I couldn't have articulated it at that time, I sensed that a permanent home, a home that would not be left in a year, or in six months, or soon, the way my family was so often on the move, deeply affected the temperaments and the activities of the family members. Both Uncle Bert and Aunty Doll's leisure and pleasure were centred in their home and garden, in maintaining and improving. A leaky tap, a faulty electric switch – Uncle Bert put them to rights as soon as he noticed them. He didn't seem to have any outside interests, except to listen to the news on the wireless and to go to union meetings at the foundry once or twice a month. Neither he nor Aunty May went to political meetings but they always voted Labour, they said. They sometimes sounded just like Mister Schmidt from downstairs in our house, saying the same kinds of things he, or my father, said about the war being a plot of the rich to make money from manufacturing arms. 'The ordinary people of every country,' Aunty Doll declared, her face flushed with fervour, 'are just that – ordinary people. French, English, Christians, Jews, or blessed Hottentots! All of them. They aren't ogres or devils. Just people, with good and bad among 'em all. They could live in peace together if their leaders didn't stir up hatreds against this, that, or t'other group.'

Dorothy Brown was proud that she knew all the words of *The Red Flag*, the Labour Party anthem, and I learned them by heart, too, joining in the singing with Aunty Doll and Colleen and Merle. I remember every word to this day:

The people's flag is deepest red.
It shrouded oft their martyred dead.
And ere their limbs were stiff and cold
Their heart's blood dyed its every fold.

So raise the scarlet banner high.
Beneath its shade we'll win or die.
Though cowards flinch and traitors sneer,
We'll keep the red flag flying here!

We sang it as lustily and joyously as members of a church congregation might sing *Onward Christian Soldiers*, with Aunty Doll waving her arms to keep time, her country-red cheeks glowing with health and warmth. I liked the way the words seemed to fit the tune, but I had no idea what they meant.

The Browns were not churchgoers – 'We don't wear our religion on our sleeves,' Aunty May told me to my confusion – and although their first child, stillborn, was buried in hallowed ground in the old graveyard at the corner of the road, the tiny, unmarked grave was overgrown and neglected. It worried me that under the small, weed-covered mound lay a tiny member of the Brown family. Colleen and Merle told me about the grave on one of our weekend walks.

'That's our baby sister, there' said Merle, still a baby herself, at seven years old. 'And I don't care if she is dead,' she continued. 'There's enough girls in our family, anyway!'

I was troubled by this as I felt the infant should be housed at least as neatly as the rest of the family.

'Can I tidy… it… up?' I asked Aunty Doll, hesitating, not quite able to say the word, 'grave.'

'You can if you like,' Aunty Doll shrugged. 'But we're not sentimental about the dead, here. We think it's the living we should care for.' She gave me a pair of garden shears, anyway, and some household scissors for trimming grass, and I cut the weeds back until the grave could be seen. All the while, I was picturing the body below as a beautiful, creamy-skinned, rosy-cheeked, golden-haired doll, lying on a pink, satin-edged shawl. I made a wooden marker and persuaded Uncle Bert to letter 'Baby Brown' with white paint. Soon, the weeds and the wild flowers grew back as dense as before, and I stopped visiting the small mound as the seasons brought more pressing activities.

Within weeks, I was speaking with the same accents I heard all around me and I began talking of my 'Moom and Dard', just as Colleen and Merle did of their parents. When I went to buy a piece of fabric for myself in one of the local shops and announced, 'I wanna buy soom stoof for a sarsh,' the saleswoman, herself a Londoner, found it hard not to laugh at my mixture of cockney and Mid-country vowels.

'Soom stoof?' she hooted. 'Soom stoof? Let's see what kinda stoof we can find for yer!'

I explained that I had been chosen to present a bouquet to the Mayor of Peterborough, who was coming to Paston to welcome the evacuees. The Mayor was to make a speech, offering hospitality to the Londoners for as long as they needed to stay.

'Aunty Doll's gonna help me make a dress,' I told the saleswoman, 'She found a piece o' lace in a drawer for the underneath part but I hafta have soomthing for a collar and sash.'

The saleswoman and I pondered the problem together, carefully considering several possibilities among the bolts of jewel-toned taffetas and satins. The saleswoman – 'You call me Aunty Marge, sweedart!' – hugged me tightly as I was about to leave the shop with my little package.

'Pretty as a pickcha, you'll be, you mark my words. Pretty as a pickcha! That mayor'll wanna take you 'ome wiv 'er!'

'Madame Mayor,' I recited for the twentieth time, practicing hard to commit my lines to memory. 'Madame Mayor. We, the children of Benthal Road School, thank you for your kind hospitality…' I accented the aspirate so I wouldn't leave it off, '…with these flowers.'

The Browns all joined in the words with me as I rehearsed, encouraging me to repeat them over and over again. All except Merle, who disappeared into her room while so much attention was being focused on me, also practiced the deep curtsy that was expected both before and after the delivery of the short speech and the presentation of the flowers. Even Uncle Bert practiced curtsying, with his lips pursed, as though kissing the air. Holding out the sides of his trouser legs, little fingers extended, he slowly lowered his large, muscular body, one foot daintily pointed in front of the other.

The occasion was a great success. I remembered my words and toppled only slightly when I curtsied. I thought I looked beautiful, as I examined my reflection in Aunty Doll's full-length bedroom mirror before I left for the school hall. My shining, freshly-washed hair was brushed into long ringlets, with some little wispy curls framing my face. My blue eyes sparkled and my cheeks and lips were made a little rosier than was altogether natural for me by the touches of rouge Aunty Doll had applied. Madame Mayor smiled serenely and kissed me on the cheek as she graciously accepted the flowers, working hard not to appear surprised at the child with the painted face, dressed in a second-hand ecru lace curtain trimmed with electric blue satin.

November brought the first light snow of the season, and my eleventh birthday. A birthday treat for the children at the Brown's was choosing the midday meal. I chose beef stew and suet dumplings, Aunty Doll's specialty, and a dish I had not tasted before coming to Paston. My mother made matzo-meal dumplings –knadels – that were served in clear chicken soup, and they were nice, too, but these suet delicacies clung to the teeth and palate with a texture as rich and satisfying as love. They came to the table bathed in dark, fruity gravy, mouth-watering to contemplate. I thought about them the whole morning at school.

My birthday post was piled by my plate – a blue card from Colleen and a green one from Merle – each painstakingly hand-made and coloured with crayons, put together secretly in their bedroom the previous week. Also by my plate, a soft, brown-paper packet held a close-fitting, dark-blue velvet bonnet and a long scarf, both liberally trimmed with fur, and also made secretly by Aunty Doll. The velvet was among the materials brought back from Peterborough. I had stroked it and smoothed it against my cheek, loving its softness, never dreaming it was for me.

The envelope from London, addressed in my father's large, elegant script I saved for last. It held a pound note tucked in the folds of an elaborately decorated and padded pink satin card inscribed, '*A Birthday Wish for a Beloved Daughter*' Inside, the printed message read:

> Our birthday wish for our dear girl,
> Is more than words can say.
> May all your dearest dreams come true
> And the sun shine on you every day.

To this, my Dad had added:

> Our darling Monica,
> We miss your smiling face more than you can ever know. We think of you by day and by night, and we are sad that you are not with us. We hope it will not be too long before we are all together again. The money is for you to spend on what ever you like. We send it to you with heartfelt love. We love you very much, darling girl.
>
> Mummy and Daddy

Reciting the words aloud, as I had read all the other greetings, I felt my throat tighten and my eyes begin to sting. I closed my eyes hard but, try as I would to hold them back, the tears forced their way down my cheeks. I pushed my chair away from the table and ran into my room, rubbing at the tears with the backs of my hands.

'Damn that man!' I could hear Uncle Bert through the wall. He sounded angry. 'Why didn't he have enough sense not to upset the child when she was settling in so well!' Aunty Doll, more understanding, argued gently. 'He wasn't to know that a sentimental message would have that effect. Birthdays are for telling people you love 'em, after all…'

'Yes, but these are not ordinary times…' Uncle Bert lowered his voice and I couldn't hear any more of the conversation until Aunty Doll's voice was raised. 'She'll get over it soon enoof. With Christmas coming, there'll be no end of things to tek 'er mind off it.'

From that day, though, my enthusiasm for learning, my excitement at every new discovery, my curiosity, began to flag. At first, my longing for home was intermittent, so that I continued to enjoy most of each day's activities.

Before Christmas of that year, 1939, I sat for 'the Scholarship' among all my London classmates. It took place in one of the larger classrooms of the Paston School. The desks were arranged in single lines, instead of being pushed together in twos, as they usually were, and every movement of the children, who were firmly forbidden to talk to each other, was monitored by a proctor. The proctor walked slowly, silently, constantly, between the rows. Even so, without fully understanding the significance of the event, it didn't seem very serious to me. Very few children our family knew, except for my brother, went on to the High School, which was what a scholarship would allow, or had any such aspirations. Most of the young people in the neighbourhood left the senior school at fourteen and were apprenticed to cabinet-makers, or tailors, or went straight on to become factory hands, or to start work at one of the garages nearby. I enjoyed answering the questions set out in the little booklet. Like puzzles, or games, they were, and I found them fascinating, writing the answers clearly in the spaces provided, my tongue poking through my lips, totally absorbed.

Preparations for Christmas were also diverting, as Aunty Doll knew they would be. Presents began arriving from the Brown's friends and relatives weeks before the holiday. Packages of all shapes, large and small, heavy and light, arrived by mail or were delivered by hand, and were soon stacked so high in the narrow front hall that no one could pass to open the front door. If there were a rat-a-tat at the front, Aunty Doll, or one of us children yelled over the packages, 'Come to the back! Please come to the back, whoever you are!'

Every delivery for the Browns included a gift for me, and I kept a tally, as did the other girls, of exactly how many parcels I would have by Christmas morning. Greetings cards were opened as they arrived and were strung on threads around the living room, beginning over the fireplace and looping around the walls in layers, hundred of cards. I had never seen anything like it. Some cards were factory-made, printed with rosy-breasted robins and sleighs and country scenes thick with frost. Some were homemade, decorated with cut-outs of Christmas trees and plum puddings topped with holly. Colleen and Merle made all the cards sent from the Browns, and they showed me how to draw green, authentically prickly-looking holly, and decorate it with shiny red berries. Aunty Doll and we girls delivered many of the cards in the evenings, after tea, carolling Christmas songs as we marched through the twilit streets. Few moments of this time were left for languishing and it was not until I climbed into bed each night, cuddling my Teddy closely, that I thought about home, and Mummy and Daddy, and cried myself to sleep.

In the early hours of Christmas morning, we children spread the gifts over the floor of the cold, front room, and opened them, one by one, so each one could be enjoyed by all. They were mostly simple, homemade items. Handkerchief sachets and pyjama cases were popular that year, as in all years, and each of us received two of each, personally monogrammed in coloured embroidery of various levels of artistry. Handkerchiefs edged with scraps of lace, suitable only for decorative purposes, and scarves of many colours made from the year's end collection of yarns, piled up among the knitted mittens and fancy gas-mask cases. I watched Colleen's presents even more closely than my own, waiting for the skates to be revealed. Colleen had been promised roller skates and had described to me exactly what they would be like.

'Will you let me ride them, Colleen? Please? Will you? Please?' I begged, so filled with envy I could hardly contain myself.

'Of course I will. You can even ride them first, if you want to.'

'Can I?' I was overwhelmed by such generosity. I wasn't sure that I could make such an offer, if I were the one expecting skates. I'd been watching the children skating in the streets and longed to skim the pavements as they did.

My surprise, when I opened my present from Aunty Doll and Uncle Bert was total. All became clear! No wonder Colleen had made that promise! She must have known all along. I threw my arms around both girls, hugging them as hard as I could. The hooting and noise and laughter brought Aunty Doll into the front room, holding her ears. But smiling.

'Do you have any idea what time it is?'

We looked up from the floor.

'It's twenty to five!'

'Is it too early to go out skating?

'Of course it is. Wait until after breakfast, at least!'

Now more subdued, we opened the remaining packages, no longer much interested in their contents. I kept turning to the skates I had placed close by on the floor, running their wheels across the palms of my hands, swooping and weaving them through the air, as though they were aircraft. As soon as the breakfast dishes were cleared away, I was out in the street, the skates adjusted and strapped to my shoes, holding onto gates, low walls, tree trunks, lamp posts, making my way gingerly across the paving slabs, struggling for balance. In an hour, I was able to skate freely, if unsteadily, along the roads. My long curls, hanging out from below the blue velvet bonnet, bounced on the shoulders of my heavy coat, the furry ends of my new scarf flying out behind me.

At midday, we all climbed onto the Peterborough bus for Christmas dinner at Uncle Bert's sister Em's house. I had never seen so much food! Roasts, and mince pies, plum puddings, and sausage rolls, rich fruit cakes, and tinned pineapple were pressed upon us, and Christmas crackers were pulled, the sharp explosions sending Aunt Em's brown terrier into frenzies of barking and squealing. Uncle Bert locked the dog in the garden shed until all that noise was over. Favours fell from the crackers, and children — first, second, and third cousins of Colleen and Merle — scurried for them on the polished linoleum. Aunts and great aunts and uncles were there, too, all including me in their questioning, just as if I had always been one of the family.

'And how old are you, now?' This was Great-Aunt Alice.

'Eleven.'

'Almost in your teens, my dear. Almost in your teens,' Colleen whispered behind me.

'Almost in your teens, my dear. Almost in your teens,' great Aunt Alice repeated, in identical cadence.

'She always says that,' Colleen whispered. 'Every year since I was six!'

We girls tittered behind our hands, the great aunt smiling with pleasure, warmed by the happy young faces, and by several glasses of after-dinner port.

Buses stopped running in the late afternoon.

'We can sleep here tonight, on the floor,' Uncle Bert offered the suggestion for our consideration. 'Or we can walk all the way home. We won't get there 'til after midnight!'

'Let's walk! Walk!' Merle shouted. 'I've never stayed up 'til midnight before. Will my clothes turn into rags?'

'No. But you might turn into a witch!' her father smiled. 'Do you think you can manage the long walk? It's a lot of miles and you're getting too big for me to carry.'

'Yes! Yes! Let's walk!'

Heavy snow had begun falling in the afternoon; it had now settled more than an inch deep and was falling faster.

We walked through the dark, deserted streets, briskly at first, with Merle trotting to keep pace, then slowing to an even, steady tread. The snow scrunched under our shoes, flew in our faces, and melted in our eyes. Without a word, we all linked hands and swung our arms between us, marching in step. After an hour or so, the snowfall lessened, and then stopped. Snow-covered roofs and paths and trees sparkled in the moonlight. Save for the crunching of the snow as we walked, the night was silent. After another hour of steady tramping, Colleen and I crossed linked hands to make a seat for Merle who, while not uttering a word of complaint, was clearly growing weary. We carried the child awkwardly between us for several hundred yards, pausing frequently to rearrange our aching hands, or lurching to one side or another as we fell out of step, until Uncle Bert lifted the youngster onto his back. She slipped her arms around his neck and was soon fast asleep, her head jogged gently by her father's steps.

By March, my longing for the home I had left behind grew into a debilitating sickness. With each letter from my mother or my father, I cried. My joy in food disappeared and even the now-minute portions Aunty Doll put on my plate were left unfinished. I'd always been a slender child but now I began to look haggard, dark patches shadowing the skin under my reddening eyes. My mother and father had come to Paston only once. Parents of evacuees were discouraged from visiting their children. It was thought unsettling for the youngsters and, although there were few signs of war in London, the government didn't want the children to begin returning there. That would surely happen, it was believed, if they saw their parents and then had to be parted from them again. Besides, it was a costly journey, and my Dad's work was intermittent, at best.

My crying fits grew more frequent, a daily event, set off by any reference, however oblique, to London, or to my parents. One day, when I was home from school for the midday meal, I began to cry as though bereaved. On the wireless, Paul Robeson was singing:

Lulla, lulla, lulla,lulla bye, bye,
Do you want the moon to play with
Or the stars to run away with.
They'll come if you don't cry
So lulla lulla lulla lulla bye, bye,
In your mammy's arms be-creeping
And soon you'll be a-sleeping
Lula, lula, lula, lula, bye.

My Mummy sang that song to me, but I'd never heard it on the air before. It was more than I could bear. I became so incapacitated by my misery that I couldn't go back to school that afternoon. Aunty Doll tucked me into bed where I lay sobbing, my face turned to the wall. 'I don't feel well,' I whimpered. 'I don't feel at all well.'

The Browns must have discussed the troubling issue of my declining health and they decided that it wouldn't hurt if I went home for visit. Bert Brown wrote to my father. He would put me on a train in Peterborough and my Dad would meet me at St Pancras. As I waved to Uncle Bert from the soot-stained window of the train, I knew that I wouldn't come back. I was never going to leave my Moom and Dard again.

In retrospect, it is dazzlingly clear that the Browns were wonderfully kind, generous, and sensitive people. They and their relatives treated me as one of their own. I could not have been in a better place – had it not been for my overwhelming longing for home.

Six

Alan Diamond's Story

Alan was very clear about the date of the day he was evacuated. 'It was 3 September, two days before my birthday. I was going to be five.' He and his family lived in London at the time, just a few blocks from Regent's Park. 'As you know, that's where the zoo is,' he told me. In 1939, he was enrolled in a church school kindergarten near St Pancras Station.

'The place we were evacuated to was a small village in Northamptonshire, about eighty miles from London. The village was two or three miles outside of Kettering.'

I asked him if he recalled much about that day.

'My memory of the day of the evacuation – it's just highlights, really. I don't have a distinct memory. I was such a little boy. I know we were not told we were going anywhere until the morning of the event and – this is rather confused in my mind – the school was evacuated en masse, as I recall. I was evacuated with five of my brothers and sisters as a group, six of us in all, because we all went to the same school. We were not evacuated with my parents. They stayed behind, as did my eldest brother and sister.'

'*Did anyone in the family see you off?*'

'I don't recall that any of them did. It would have been really upsetting I think, if they had – and I would remember that. We kids just all walked to the school together, as we'd been told to do.'

'*Tell me a bit about your family,*' I asked him. '*Were you the youngest?*'

'No, the ages ranged from the youngest one, my youngest brother, Leonard, who was eighteen months younger than me. That would make him three and a half. And the eldest was my sister, one of my other sisters, not the one who stayed home. She would have been about thirteen.'

'When we arrived in a small village, which was after a journey by train and by bus, all of us were taken to a village hall and there we were sort of dumped in one big lump. I don't recall any of the meals we were given, although I'm sure they gave us sandwiches. That first night, we stayed in the village hall and we had palliasses, like made up straw mattresses, and we slept on those mattresses the first night. We'd never experienced anything like that before.'

When I asked Alan how the children were assigned to billets, he said:

'I don't know how they chose the children for billeting. There seemed to be people coming and going and taking kids away and, eventually, I was sent outside this village to some other village, and my younger brother – that would be the one who was three and a half – was sent with another sister who was ten and a half, to another house. And my next eldest brother was sent to another house. But how they decided this, I have no idea.'

'*So the whole family was split up? How many? Six of you altogether, did you say?*' I asked.

'We were eight children in the family in all, and two of them were left behind, so, yes, there were six of us evacuated together.'

'*Can you recall what kind of schooling you had while you were away?*'

'Well, there were two schools in the village. One was like a kindergarten, which took children up to six years old. Then, for ages six through eleven there was like an elementary school. As I was five years old that coming school term, I did go to the kindergarten. I had regular fulltime schooling in the kindergarten for one year and then, for the rest of the years, I moved over into the elementary school and I just went through a complete school program.'

'*Were you in the same household for the whole time, too?*'

'Oh, no. I had several billets. I'll start at the beginning.' He paused, brow furrowed, as he assembled the order of the placements in his mind. 'The first place I went to was a butcher's shop and they had two young boys there of my own age. I have very fond memories of that place. I seemed to fit in very well and I would have been quite content to stay there for the duration. But the powers that be decided that we should be kept together as a family. Nobody asked me.' His emphasis indicated his resentment, felt even after so many years, of being pushed around like a pawn in a board game whose rules were unfathomable.

'So, the first place was during a kind of a shake-down period. I was there for only a couple of months, and then I was taken from there and put with my sister and younger brother. So that was my second placement. Actually, the second billet was okay, too. There were the three of us there and those people were also very good to us. We were there for only a few months, though – maybe six months – and then we were split up again.' He sighed. There was more to come.

'The next billet I went to with just my sister. There was this lady – she was a very strange person. I don't think she understood children at all. Or she was taking children in out of a sense of patriotism, or maybe just because there was some small payment involved, because I got the feeling she really didn't want us there. We were never ever physically abused but this lady engaged in what I would call a form of mental abuse. Not to a great degree, but the subtlety was there and, as a child, I knew it was there. She was just so cold.' He shuddered as he brought the woman to mind. 'I got no sense of warmth from this person – especially when I went through a series of childhood illnesses during the time we were in that house – German measles and such. I can see that it must have been a pain in the neck for the lady, who became especially sour when I was confined to bed. And then, after another few months, we were moved again, and I can't say I was sorry this time.'

Once more, Alan and just one sister were re-housed. The youngest of the boys, still an infant really, had been taken back to London. Alan's older sister, too, had gone back to London. She had turned fourteen and was out of the school system.

'We were in the fourth place for a while. In that billet, there were children from other families, so there were about four or five of us. It was okay, but then we moved from there to another lady's house. My little brother who had gone back to London returned to the village because of the air raids.' Then the little brother and Alan were billeted together in a fifth place that they really liked, 'but the lady was moving to Scotland. She wanted to take me with her – and I would love to have gone. I was always ready for an adventure – but my mother didn't want me to be that far from London. So, when the lady left, I went to the sixth, or fifth lady – I've lost count.' He shook his head, wanting to get the facts right, but he had been just a small child at that time and the details were difficult to put in order. 'And I was with her for three years, right to the end of the war. I stayed in that village until the actual end of the war in Europe. I remember being home for Easter of 1945.'

'Did you ever go back to London for a visit during all those years away?'

'Yes, I did go back for a very short time. It must have been 1943 or 1944. There had been a lull in the raids on London. I was always asking my parents, "When can I come home, when can I come home?" I must say they did make a visit to the village every month. They did make that effort to be with us, and, if I could digress for a minute, I found that more disturbing than helpful. I felt as though I was being pulled between two lives all the time. Every time they'd come down, it would awaken old memories and I'd want to come home. Eventually, they said "yes, you can come home" as the air raids had stopped. I went back for the two week school holiday period over Easter and, unfortunately for me, that's when some of the air raids started up again. The first night I was there, we had this tremendous air raid and I was extremely frightened. I had come from this very quiet village where nothing happened after nine o'clock, and I was thrust into this terrifying experience. Also, London had changed. If you remember, I had left before the bombing had started and the phoney war was about the begin, and I remembered my family as being a small, unified group. When I went back, I found that the family was spread all over the place. My eldest brother was in the army, one of my sisters was working night shift at one of the factories, and it was just not as I remembered.

All of this was traumatizing, and I had no preparation for it. Out there in the country, we had no idea what had been going on in London. The night of that air raid, all I can remember were the sirens and the fires. There was a tremendous number of fires. The sky was blood red, that's the only way I can describe it. And I can remember just running down the street to the shelter, with the anti-aircraft guns, which were right there in Regents Park, going off like every second it seemed. My father was holding one of my brothers, and my mother had one of my other brothers by the hand, and I was like the third child there. Luckily, my older brother, who was on leave from the army, grabbed me and ran down to the shelter with me. You can't imagine what it was like being crammed into the shelter with all those other people, the smell of damp concrete was the most powerful smell I can remember, together with strong disinfectant, and the way the shelter shook as each bomb exploded somewhere nearby and as the guns went off in the park. I went back to the country the next day! I couldn't wait to get out of London!'

'*You seem to be reliving that terrible night,*' I commented, watching the way his face registered his fear.

'Yes. I have lived through it over and over again. One of the lasting effects of just that brief period in London has been a form of claustrophobia, which then developed at some point into slight agoraphobia, that manifests itself as fear-panic attacks without having any rational basis for them. I've been through a lot of therapy trying to resolve this. Successfully, I think, to a large degree I still have problems, however, and I still try to avoid flying, although I have flown, of course. I'm particularly affected by jet flying.'

Quietly, over a cup of tea, Alan told me about his lasting sense of dislocation.

'One other effect of the evacuation,' he pondered, 'is that I never have a sense of belonging anywhere. I'm not sure if I came from London, or whether I came from the village. Was I from the country? And having been in so large a number of houses and families over those years, I just have, I still have, this feeling that I truly don't belong anywhere at all, whether it be London or Los Angeles, where I've lived for a few years – except in the country. That's where I feel that perhaps I do belong. I could pick up from Los Angeles tomorrow and leave – and I have good memories of Los Angeles, but I don't consider it as a home, a place where I need to be, need to stay. And I've had this feeling as long as I can remember.'

'*Is it all gloom, though?*' I asked him. '*Were there no benefits to balance the costs?*'

'Well, yes. I think one of the positive sides of this experience is that it did take me out of a working class family. It did show me that there are other paths you can travel in the world. I have learned to take advantage of opportunities as they have come along. I think that if I had stayed in London with my family, in that environment, if the war hadn't happened, I would not be where I am today, as a respected professional.' He paused briefly, as though considering whether he had said anything inappropriate or ungrateful. 'Don't get me wrong, though, I loved my family. I still love them.'

'Can you tell me, then, how you felt, leaving your family in London?'

'Well, even today, I can't express my feelings all that clearly. I don't quite know what they were. It's part of the ongoing process of trying to figure out what happened to me during that time. I do know that not being told what was happening was the worst thing that happened to me then. I mean, nobody did any preparation. We were dressed in our Sunday best and sent off. I knew that something was wrong. My brother – my next eldest brother – tells a story of how my father was crying when we were sent away. He did not want us to go, although he'd been through the First World War, when the Zeppelins were bombing London, and he knew what to expect.'

'I was very strongly attached to my father, He was a truly supportive and wonderful person and I really missed him when I was away from him. I missed the rest of my family, too. Not so much my mother, because my mother had – I think she was pregnant at the time with my youngest brother and I don't think she was a happy woman. She may have had some emotional problems. Perhaps not serious problems. I think she was frustrated. She had just too many children and too much work to do. So I was really raised by my elder sister, Alice. But being broken away from the support of the sisters and brothers was the hardest thing for me – and when Alice didn't come away with us, that wasn't good. I didn't like that. I missed her particularly.'

'Still, there were some things about the country life and the evacuation that seem to have stayed with you through your life.'

'Yes.' His face brightened. 'There were some positives from being in the country. First of all, I was exposed to things I never knew existed. The last people I was with for the longest time, Mr and Mrs Smith – Mr Smith was a great gardener. He would always win the chrysanthemum show, the best potato, the best tomato. He took such pride in doing things well. And, although I was too young to help him in the garden, he encouraged me to be an observer. So I developed a love for the country and growing things and this connection with the earth.

My father was also very appreciative of the country. He would come out on his monthly visit and smell the air and say "This is wonderful!" and there was never any competition with Mr Smith over what he was doing. Between the pair of them, I was able to develop the love for the country that I still have today. That's probably where I'll go to retire, if I ever do. I'll leave the big city and start planting things for myself.' He smiled at the thought. And shrugged.

Seven

Stella Stern's Story

'Can you imagine!' Stella began, 'I was three years old and my "grown-up" big sister was seven, maybe eight, and there we were, two little tots, going down to the school with our gas masks and a few of our possessions – clothes and so on – in a bag, and being told to line up with the other children. We walked off to the railway station, two by two, like the animals boarding Noah's Ark, and onto a train we climbed, not knowing where we were going or what was happening. At the very least, we were apprehensive and, I'm sure, terribly scared. My sister felt very responsible for me and she helped me up the step onto the train and she hardly let go of my hand for the whole journey.'

'But didn't your mother take you to school and see you off? What was the story there?'

'No, she couldn't. We were living with our grandparents at the time. My father was in the army and my mother was with him. We just walked by ourselves down to the school with our little bit of luggage. We surely weren't able to carry much. The school must have been quite close to the house.'

'Where were you living at that time?'

'Our grandparents lived in Shoeburyness, Southend-on-Sea, on the Channel, right across the water from France. So I suppose it was wise to get us out of there as quickly as possible. I'm told that guns were quickly set up on the beaches there, and that the Kursal (an entertainment centre) was shut down, and the town was soon filled with uniformed soldiers. Only six months or so later, the end of May and the beginning of June 1940 – and of course I didn't learn about this until I was much older – all kinds of motor yachts were requisitioned, ordered to go to Southend Pier with volunteer crews to stock up with fuel and provisions. Then they were to head off to Dunkirk to help in the evacuation of thousands of British and Dutch troops, and bring them back to England. All the while, the boats were being bombarded from the air. So it's just as well we left when we did.'

'*Can you remember where you went or much about it? You were just a tiny child.*'

'Well, I now know that it was a little town called Ashbourn, in Derbyshire. When we got there, we were taken off the train and put on a bus. I'm not sure how far we went but when we all got off the bus, we were led to the local church hall. When we arrived there, we were told to sit outside on a hill where all of us were to wait until local people came and selected the children they would be taking out to their homes. What I remember most clearly was that my sister and I were holding hands and everybody was trying to split us up and we refused to let go of each other, so we were the last children sitting there. It was late at night and it was getting dark. Finally, it seemed that one couple, who said they didn't really want two children but being that the two of us seemed to be inseparable, they would accept the two of us. So that's how we got to our first adopted home.'

'*What do you recall about the family who took you in?*'

'Well, he was the local postman and it was – how can I describe them – a very respectable family. The house and the garden were well-kept, neat and clean. They had brought up two children, now grown, and they were very strict with us. We were never able to eat with the family. They sat at the dining table and we had to stay in the kitchen. They may have thought we'd spill things and make a mess, being as we were so young.'

'*So you were hardly treated like one of the family?*'

'Oh no, not at all. I do remember very well that when the daughter got married, we – my sister and I – were given sandwiches and we were sent to the park. It was a very wet, cold day, and we sat there all day long with our sandwiches because, for some reason that I still can't fathom, we were not allowed to go and attend the wedding. When the rain got really heavy, and our clothes were getting soaked through, someone came out from the reception and sat us in one of their cars. I suppose we were lucky that they remembered where we were! In the evening, we were picked up and taken back to the house, damp and hungry.

I've often wondered about those people. What could they have been thinking? After we were at their house for just one month, I think they must have decided that they'd taken on too much with two of us and they decided to give us to the hostel. We took all our things and they walked us up to this place – it's all really vague in my mind – and they left us there. I think it must have been a kind of an orphanage, but I'm not really sure… A few days later, they came and took us back to their house. I've never been able to understand what that was about. It could be that the couple was having marital problems? I've almost given up trying to understand it – but I do still ponder over it sometimes.'

'*Earlier, you described them as "very respectable". Were these religious people? What can you recall about that?*'

'They were religious. They belonged to the Church of England and their son was the lead man in the choir. He carried the cross in the procession and yes, they were very good, Christian people. We were made to go to Sunday school and we went to church every Sunday, even though we were Jewish. I do remember that very clearly.'

'*How did you feel about going to church? That was not what you were used to, was it?*'

'Well, no, but I didn't really know any other kind of religion at that point because I was only three years old. So, although I was born to a Jewish family, I was brought up as Church of England, and I didn't know of any other faith until I was returned to London at the end of the war.'

'*Did you go to school while you were away?*'

'We did go to school, or, we sort of went to school. We evacuees were kept separate from the local children and we had classes in this Sunday school hall, which I remember being divided down the middle. Half of the children were on one side of the room and half were on the other side. We were probably separated by age. We had two teachers, one on each side of the hall, and that was the extent of our schooling. We never mingled with the local children, and we never had the feeling that we belonged to the community.'

'*How long were you away altogether?*'

'I was away for six years.'

'*That would seem like the entire duration of the war. Was your sister with you the whole of that time?*'

'Actually, my sister went back to London when she was about thirteen or so, going on fourteen, and they felt she was old enough to be returned to home – our grandparents had left Southend and moved to London by that time. It seems that my sister could no longer be considered an evacuee. I think there was some kind of an age that they thought the child should be returned to the family?'

'*Are you talking about your family's wishes here, or was it the authorities that made this decision?*'

'Oh, it was the authorities, I'm sure. It was getting towards time for her to be leaving school. My family surely would have thought it wiser for her to stay out of harm's way.'

'*While your sister was evacuated, was she in the same billet with you the whole time?*'

'No, we were together for a couple of years, I think, and then she went to live with another family. I just remember that she had to do a lot of housework for her keep in the house we were in together. She used to have to scrub the floors. She really worked hard at that house. I'll never forget that. I think that some of the host families thought they could treat the evacuees, especially the bigger girls, as unpaid servants. Of course, there's nothing wrong with children being encouraged to keep their rooms tidy and make their beds and all that, but scrubbing floors on their hands and knees does seem a bit harsh. Actually, one of the girls who came away with us was treated so badly she never wanted to go back to that house, and they had to find another place for her to stay.'

'*Did your sister experience the bombing when she went back to London?*'

'Unfortunately for her, she went back just as the flying bombs were starting in London – the buzz bombs – and this caused her, to this day, to be a very nervous person, very high strung and jumpy. It really was a bad time for her to be in London and she remembers the terrible feeling of knowing that these bombs could fly in at any minute. It was nerve-wracking for her – and for everyone else who had to put up with it. You just didn't know when these bombs were going to drop or where they were going to land, so people were constantly being shuttled to the shelters. I feel lucky that I didn't have to go through the same experiences.'

'*You were a very little girl when you went away and you were away for a very long time. How did you feel when you went home and returned to your mother at the end of the war?*'

'It felt very strange, and it took a long time to get used to having her with me. What I felt at first was that my mother had deserted me because of the war, and I couldn't understand why she had not been down to the country to take me home. Now, all these years later, I realise that when my mother said it was the safest place for us to have been, she was right and she was only thinking of what was best for us. Obviously, for my sister, it would have been the best place for her to be until the war finished, but she had no choice. Actually, when I went home, I didn't stay long with my mother, who had moved to Lancashire by then, but I went back to live in my grandparents' home in London. I was emotionally a lot closer to them than to my parents.'

'*There were obviously some negative aspects to the evacuation for you that you have been telling me about, but you said that you also have some positive memories.*'

'Among my most positive memories were, first of all, getting to see the beautiful countryside around Derbyshire. It was such a pleasure! I'm sure I would never have seen that part of the country if it weren't for the evacuation. I got to visit the farms, I got to see how people lived in the little villages, I got to understand people outside of London. I got a very good education on how people lived in the countryside as against people in the city. So, it was a learning period, too. I might not have had this – surely would not have had this, had there not been a war. On Saturday mornings, we'd go to the local farmer's market, and I would marvel at all the lovely colourful fresh vegetables, and the live chickens and the animals that were for sale. And on Saturday afternoons, we went to the cinema, which was always a treat. And, although there was an airdrome nearby, as far as I know, there were no bombs dropped in Derby. I was able to live my life away from the war, for which I am truly thankful.'

'We thought we were going on a holiday'. (Image courtesy of Associated Press)

Off they went, with their gas masks and their packages. (Image courtesy of the Imperial War Museum, London)

Off on the train, 1940. (Image courtesy of the Imperial War Museum, London)

Evacuees leaving Stepney, 1939. (Image courtesy of the Imperial War Museum, London)

Children leaving from the East End of London, 2 September 1939.
(Image courtesy of the Imperial War Museum, London)

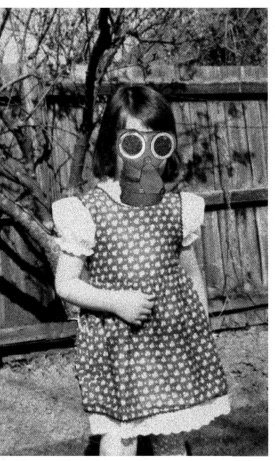

How a litttle girl wearing a gas mask would have appeared.. (Diz White Images)

My old, threadbare Teddy. (Diz White Images)

DRAWING BY DIZ WHITE

Children gather at school for the evacuation, 1939. (The Monica B. Morris Archives)

Evacuees and teachers prepare to board the train. (The Monica B. Morris Archives)

Evacuees and teachers; Theford, Norfolk, 1939. (The Monica B. Morris Archives)

The author, evacuated to Paston, Peterborough, sent her school photograph to her parents, 1939. (The Monica B. Morris Archives)

A village view typical of those greeting the evacuees. (Diz White Images)

A village typical of those greeting the evacuees. (Diz White Images)

The author, aged ten, a few days before the evacuation, August 1939. (The Monica B. Morris Archives)

The author, with Ann Portnoy from the basement flat, in the garden a few days before the evacuation, August 1939. (The Monica B. Morris Archives)

Eight

Betty Winehouse's Story

Betty and I began our conversation by sharing our memories of life just before the announcement that Britain was at war with Germany.

'*Do you remember when the blackout started?*' I asked her.

'Oh, I remember that very clearly' she said. We were told that on 1 September, 1939 the streets were going to go black. We had to keep all our curtains closed and, later on, we had to tape the windows with brown paper tape to prevent the shattering of the glass. But this first night, on September the first, we went outside and the street lights were on. Then, suddenly, everything went black. It was a terrible feeling because it was a dark night and there was no moon. As I remember, it was really very dark, pitch black. We lived on just an ordinary street – and there was not a light to be seen anywhere. Later on, air raid wardens would come around from time to time, to see if there were any lights showing through the curtains. If they did see one, they'd yell "Put that bloody light out!" in no uncertain terms. And if you didn't do it immediately, they'd come knocking on the door and demand "Turn that light out, missus!" But, of course, I was evacuated to the country the next day.'

'*Tell me as much as you can about that. Where did you live at that time, and where did you go.*'

'My home was in London, in Hackney, and my school, Lauriston Road, was quite near to where we lived. I was taken to Norfolk, on the East Coast, to a small village called Foulden, about eight miles from Thetford. I was thirteen years old, so I remember everything pretty clearly. It was right at the beginning of the war and I don't think that people were really ready. And I don't think people were prepared to accept us in the country.'

'*How did you get to Thetford? Can you recall?*'

'Yes, I'll never forget it. We were all taken to a railway station – Liverpool Street, I think – and from there, each class was taken separately. We were all bunched together at the station, carrying our gas masks and one small piece of luggage. Some had little suitcases, some had their things in carrier bags. Our parents did not see us off, only our teachers were with us. From the station, we got on the train to Thetford, and from Thetford, we were taken by bus to individual places to stay.'

'*How were the billets assigned?*'

'Well, we were all in a school hall. I remember it was quite late in the evening by the time everyone had assembled, and the people who were going to take us came into the hall and quite literally just chose who they wanted. I was billeted in a couple of places over time.'

'*Where did you go first? Who picked you from the school hall?*'

'They were rather an adult couple. I remember the lady had silver hair but I don't think she was very old. He was a farm worker and they had two sons. One was sixteen and the other one was eleven or twelve. They lived in a beautifully clean little house, but the woman, apparently, was not too well. Well, I was a big girl at thirteen, tall and slim, and I suppose she thought – she actually told me that she wanted me to help her in the house. She made it quite clear that I would do housework and digging in the garden. She obviously thought I was going to be a kind of a maid to her. I didn't mind that so much, but pretty soon I had a problem with the sixteen-year-old son.

'He…' She hesitated, trying to find appropriate words. 'He… molested me. He kept touching me on my breasts and, at thirteen years at that time, well, I was absolutely horrified that he touched me, and it was very difficult for me to deal with. I was completely naïve; I knew absolutely nothing about sex at that time and it was altogether shocking to me.'

'*Did you tell anybody about this?*'

'I told a teacher and I said I can't have this happening to me and would he move me somewhere else. You can imagine how embarrassing it was for me to talk to a man teacher about such a personal thing. Anyway, he arranged for me to move.'

'And the next place? How did you fare there?'

'At the next place, the couple were a shepherd and his wife. It was truly rural where they were. They had a little boy of about three years old who was a real little brat. It was a cold place and not very clean. The woman was slovenly and I didn't like it there one bit. I had a problem with the man… If I can explain: Jewish people, during the war, if they didn't eat bacon, they could have extra margarine. I had that kind of ration book that said 'extra margarine' and the man asked me "Why do you have extra margarine instead of bacon?" and I said "It's because I'm Jewish."

'From that moment on, he started calling me "Jew" and saying "Jews are heathens! All Jews are heathens!" Well, at thirteen years old, when you hear that, especially in those days, you didn't know how to answer back. He frightened the life out of me! And I just burst into tears every time he said it – and he said it whenever our paths crossed – which was often. Again, that was really traumatic for me and I was very upset and very unhappy there. Further, there was nothing for me to do except stay around the house. It was a difficult and unpleasant time for me.'

'Did you tell your parents about this, or your teachers?'

'Well, it happened this way. By the time I was really at my wits' end, my father came down to visit me and I met him by the front fence and I just absolutely refused to go back into the house. I told him about the shepherd and I said "Dad, you've got to take me home. I don't care what happens." My father was not eager to take me back but finally, he saw he had to. I'd been there for probably a few months, and while I was there, that's when I began putting on my weight for life!' She laughed, wryly. 'I got very heavy and I'm sure it all stems from that terribly difficult time.'

'Why do you think these people took in evacuees when they were clearly not so happy to do so?'

'It was badly arranged, to my mind. I believe they did get paid a certain amount from the government to take children in, and I don't think things were worked out really well. It was all done so quickly and, in the rural areas, people were glad to get a few extra shillings, whatever it was they got for doing that. They just said they'd take them in, no matter what the situation was. In retrospect, I can see that they were so poor. The money must have made a difference.'

'*How long were you away altogether?*'

'It wasn't all that long. Six months, maybe.'

'*So you weren't away for very long. Can you remember anything particular happening when you got back to London?*'

'Oh yes. We moved in April, 1940, to Clapton, not too far away from Hackney but a slightly better area, I think. Not too long after that, the air raids started. We were living in newer flats, and they had built shelters below the ground. We used to go down to the shelters every night. They were equipped with bunks. I must say that there was a lovely feeling amongst the people, no matter who they were. I never felt any anti-Semitism down there. Everybody was so friendly with each other that it seemed like a good time, in a way, that brought all kinds of people together… although there was the bombing, which was pretty bad.'

'*Did your house, or anyone you knew, get bombed?*'

'Yes. In fact, the block of flats we lived in was a huge 'U' shape and we were at one end of the 'U'. The other end had a landmine fall on it, and a whole slice of the building got demolished. But there was something humorous about it, because two things happened: The first was that a woman landed in the crater in her bed and she was absolutely unhurt. It was a kind of miracle, really. Can you imagine! The bed must have sailed out of her flat and landed right side up, with her still tucked under the blankets! The second thing was, my father always hung his trousers on the bedpost, and they got blown out of the window by the blast – and instead of him taking another pair of trousers, he ran downstairs in his underpants to get his trousers back. I thought that was absolutely hilarious.' She laughed at the memory, still as amused as she had been as the teenager she was at that time. 'Actually, though, it was a very bad time to be in London. I got a slight injury on my wrist from the flying glass; I carry the scar to this day. And my sister was a baby, about six months old at the time, and my mother used to put an asbestos sheet on the top of her cot to protect her. After that particular raid, there was an immense shard of glass that had got lodged in this sheet. I know, had that not been there, my sister would have been killed.'

'With all the moving from place to place, there must have been some disruption in your education. Can you tell me what kind of schooling you had during this whole time?'

'Well, unfortunately, I didn't have any schooling at all from the time the war broke out. There was a school in the village but I think there was a shortage of teachers or something, because I did not go to school. In fact, the teacher that took us down to the country asked me if I would help him to teach the younger children. I can remember teaching them "the cat sat on the mat" and how to spell simple words and things like that. But I, personally, did not go to school. I think they weren't prepared for us. The time that I was there, which was maybe six months in all, I just didn't get any schooling at all. And back in London, the schools were closed. Fortunately, the schooling I'd had before the war was pretty good. I could read and write very well and, in fact, I later went to secretarial school and I've been a secretary all my working life. For the past ten years, I've been a doctor's secretary. If I had been a little child when the war broke out, it might have been a different story if my schooling stopped, but at thirteen, nearly fourteen, I'd already absorbed a good deal in school. Thank goodness!'

'There were certainly some negative aspects to your being evacuated – so negative that you couldn't wait to get home, even though "home" might be a dangerous place to be. But wasn't there anything positive about the experience?' I asked.

'Absolutely! The really positive part of it was that I developed such a deep love of the country. I liked the open feeling. And the man in the first place I went to, the husband of the couple, worked on a farm. He used to take me with him to work occasionally, and I used to walk around the farm and help a little bit. And I just absolutely adored the village. It was so pretty with its quaint houses and lovely trees – forests, really – and all surrounded by lush fields. Foulden is actually recorded in the Domesday Book as "Fugalduna". It means "hills frequented by birds". There hasn't been much development there and the population is still minute – less than 500, and it is still very rural. There was a little shop there that I liked and, from that time, I've really loved the country. In fact, I loved it so much that, later on, I joined what was known as the Women's Land Army. So I worked on the land when I was seventeen years old and I found it fascinating, and I felt privileged to be able to work in the countryside…'

She paused, obviously wanting to tell me more, but hesitant. '*Do go on, please!*' I encouraged.

'Well, I have a really romantic story… It's a good thing you found me when you did because at the end of the week I'm going back to Norfolk to be married.' She smiled broadly, a light blush transforming her face. She was seventeen, again, the past many decades erased by her joy.

'When I was in the Land Army, I met a young farmer, not much older than myself, and we fell madly in love – you know how you do when you're that age – but we knew it was the real thing and that we would get married and live happily ever after. Well, it was not to be.'

'*Why was that? It sounds perfect.*'

'We thought so, but my father did not! When he heard about it, he went nearly mad. He came down to see me and he shouted, "If that young man comes anywhere near you again, I, personally, will break his neck! I'll kill him!" He frightened us both out of our lives!'

'*Well, you were quite young – and you would have needed his permission to get married if you were under twenty-one. But his reaction does sound rather extreme.*'

'It was nothing to do with my age. It was because the young man – William – was not Jewish. At that time, mixed marriages were pretty well unthinkable. If you married "out" your family would disown you. In more "observant" families, you would quite literally be dead to them. They would actually sit in mourning for you and never see you again. So my marriage to William was unthinkable. I was devastated. But life goes on.'

'*So is it William you are going to marry. Surely he married someone else? A farmer needs a wife…*' I wanted to know more.

'Yes! Yes, he married and had a large family, six children, all grown up now. His wife died about a year and a half ago, and somehow he managed to find me. When he heard that I was alone – I was divorced after a marriage that lasted only a few years – he said he wanted to see me. He actually came up to London, where I was at the time, and as soon as we laid eyes on each other, it was as though the years rolled right back. Eventually, I met his children. They were all very nice and welcoming to me. One of the daughters told me that her parents had been contented together and they'd had a good marriage, but the children all knew about me. They had been told about the land girl their dad had loved and how he always thought about me. It was the children who encouraged him to look for me. And there aren't any obstacles, now. Even if my dad was still alive, I think he would be happy for me. Times have changed.'

'*I'm really glad for you, and I'm fascinated that it was exposure to the countryside when you were an evacuee that led you back to the land – and back to your first love!*'

Nine

Manning M's Story

'I was twelve and a half years old when I was evacuated, and I remember it was 3 September and I believe it was a Saturday. We were all assigned to a school and I must add that it was not my school. I accompanied my little brother, who was only six years old at the time, and I was to be responsible for him. We went from Lauriston Road School, his school. Mine was the Jewish Free School and I have no idea where those students went.'

'We lived in Hackney, then, in a big block of new council flats. All the kids dispersed to their individual schools with their gas masks and their luggage, and from there they were taken by bus and by train. In our case, the train took us to Thetford, a small town in Norfolk.

'*Do you remember much about that day?*'

'At the beginning, I didn't feel much at all, except that the whole thing was rather a lark, but I'm sure I can remember my mother waving us goodbye as we boarded the bus at the school to go the local railway station. I didn't realise the seriousness of the event. It wasn't until later that I learned from my mother that she and my dad thought they might never see us again. I don't really recall much about the journey as such, but I do remember arriving at Thetford and being given something to eat, and there were toilet facilities set up.'

'*How did the town look to you?*'

'When we got out of the train at Thetford, it was just like being in a foreign country. I had a strange feeling of being in totally unfamiliar territory. I had never heard of the town before; I didn't even know what country I was in. The place was completely different from the area in which I lived. Of course, I learned a lot about Thetford later on. It's the birthplace of Thomas Paine – 1737, if I remember correctly – and there are lots of memorials to him in the town, and a pub named for him, and so on. People there are very proud of their native son. Decades later, I read Paine's *The Rights of Man*, and how I wished I had known about him while I was near his birthplace! I could have gained an education just from studying him! At least I would have learned something while I was away! I think the people I stayed with either didn't know what an illustrious man came from their area, or they simply didn't care.'

'*What happened to you after your arrival in Thetford?*'

'We milled about for a little while – it was all a bit chaotic – until they organized the buses which then transported us to the many different villages to which we were assigned. That had presumably been arranged in advance of our getting there. Two villages lay close by. One was called Little Cressingham and one was Great Cressingham. I think we went to Little Cressingham first. My brother and I were placed in the local village hall where people came and selected the children they wanted. We waited and waited for a long time. We were among the last children to be chosen, perhaps because of the main objective, which was that we were not to be separated. That was the whole point of my going away with my brother's school. I know we were very, very tired. The selection process had taken so long and it was about nine o'clock at night before we were finally found a billet.'

'*You mentioned that you were at more than one billet. What can you say about the first place?*'

'We were chosen by a family – a husband and wife with a couple of children but I can't remember a whole lot about that first billet because we were there for only about two weeks, and then we were moved. Why we were moved, and what instituted that move, I simply do not know. But we were then on our way to the second place. This was in Great Cressingham where, at that point, we lost all connection with my brother's school. We were then put into a private catholic school, also evacuated from our neighbourhood in London. It was located in Mare Street, not far from our flats, and the teachers from that school supervised us and gave us instruction for a while.'

'*What was the second billet like, and how long were you there?*'

'It was on a farm and it was pretty miserable. The farmer and his wife lived in the house with us. A daughter, a son-in-law, and a grandchild lived nearby. The son-in-law worked for the farmer as a kind of farm labourer. The two-storied farmhouse was rather simple. There was no electricity and no indoor toilet. Cooking was done on a fire with a stove behind it that heated the water. I slept with my brother in an upstairs bedroom – icy cold in the winter months. We were glad we had each other to generate a bit of heat between us. Brrrr!' He laughed as he recalled those cold nights.

'Unfortunately, we were not treated well. As I said, it was a farm and there was plenty of good food to hand: eggs and milk and butter and chickens – but we were definitely malnourished. We were given very little to eat. I remember we'd get beetroot in vinegar on bread for an evening meal. We both lost a tremendous amount of weight in the year that we were there. When I had left home, I was a real chubby boy and when my mother came to visit at the end of that year she was appalled at our appearance. I was like a skinny, scraggy chicken, she said, and she quickly arranged a move for us. When we went back for our belongings, they were outside the front door on the step and we didn't go into the house again.'

'*How do you think the local people felt about the evacuees?*'

'I can't speak for all the local people. Clearly, some felt very positive and others felt we were simply invaders and resented us, and resented that they had to share their schools with us. We all lost out on our education, not just the evacuees.'

'*Do you think the people you stayed with also resented you?*'

'I think we were just there because of the money they got. It wasn't a lot but in terms of adding to their financial resources, they must have found it useful. I think they got something like 10*s* 6*d* for the first child and 8*s* 6*d* for the second – and they made sure they made a profit out of it, to judge by the food they doled out to us – or didn't dole out to us!'

'*Were you expected to do chores on the farm?*'

'Oh, I became a regular little farm hand.' His face brightened with pleasure at the question. 'I cleaned out the horses' stables, I milked cows, I fed pigs. None of these things would I ever have done at home in Hackney! I must say, I enjoyed it quite well. There was something really comforting about burrowing my head in the side of the cow and getting the milk to gush into a bucket. Blossom, my favourite cow was called. I'll always remember Blossom! There are not too many opportunities to milk cows in Hackney! I did like the smell in the cow shed, and in the barn, too – like sweet apples mixed with hay. I think they may have stored the apple harvest up in the hayloft. And collecting eggs from the hen house was quite rewarding, too. We had mesh baskets and we would fill them with these lovely big brown eggs. If only they'd given us some of those eggs to eat! I worked particularly hard during harvest season. A friend of mine who was billeted at the rectory came to help the farmer at that time. He was given sixpence for his efforts but, of course, I was given nothing, not even a decent supper! Apart from working us quite hard and not feeding us, they also treated us very strictly. We were forced to take walks on a Sunday afternoon in all weathers, and we had to be out for several hours and not return until close to bedtime. Simply put, they wanted us out of their way. It being a fairly small village, there wasn't really anything much to do or any place to go, so we used to mill around by the local church.'

'I remember I had to go home in February of 1940 for my barmitzvah, just after I turned thirteen. One of my presents was a dressing gown, a nice woolen plaid one with silk cords – you know the kind, probably from Marks & Spencers – and when I got back with it, the farmer's wife wouldn't let me wear it! I was really upset but when I think about it now, I suppose it was rather out of place, a fancy dressing gown in a place that didn't even have an indoor toilet. Ludicrous, really!' He laughed.

'We felt really isolated there in some ways and, yet, it was a mixed experience. The farmer did take me to the local market on market day. That was in Dereham, about eight miles away, and I found that very interesting. On the other hand, something I'll remember about the evacuation to my dying day was my first experience of anti-Semitism. I was really shocked to have the word "Jew" thrown in my face. It's something that has stayed with me all these years. Also, the brother-in-law really resented us. On one occasion, he was giving my brother and me what was supposedly a treat. He was giving us a ride on the hay cart across the fields. We were on top of a high load of hay and as we turned into the field, he deliberately guided the wheel into a dip so we would fall off. He did this to show his contempt for us. You might ask why he wanted to show such contempt. He disliked us London kids; he disliked Jews, and he felt we were intruders. Going to school a few days later, I bumped into the son-in-law again, taking his boy to school, and that's when he shouted "Jew!" at me. I can still feel the humiliation I felt then. After all, there's nothing much a boy can do to retaliate against a brawny grown man under those circumstances.'

'*You've hinted that you didn't get much in the way of schooling while you were away. What happened?*'

'Well, I think my education suffered considerably. It's a little vague in my mind but I do remember that, eventually, we had to share the facilities of the local village school and there wasn't a lot of learning taking place at that time. It was a matter of getting the kids there and keeping them occupied. I must say that, ironically, even though I had left my own school to be with my brother, we were moved from school to school to school, and while some of the teachers were simply wonderful and caring and surely tried to do their best for us, I have to say that my education really came to an end in September 1939.'

'*After you left the farm, how were you treated in the next place you lived?*'

'The new family was delightful. It comprised a farm labourer, his wife, and two small children. Their name was Palmer, and they lived in small terraced country house. They gave us nice meals and we were well cared for. They also had no electricity. I remember lighting the oil lamps at night. They were most generous and kind and we were made to feel like members of their family. In fact, other members of their family also befriended us, so we didn't feel so isolated there. I had my bike there and I took my brother to school on the cross bar. We were there for only eight months and then I turned fourteen and had to leave school and, presumably, go back to London. Instead, my mother found a place for our whole family to stay in Baldock, in Hertfordshire. She knew we had to be away from the worst of the bombing. I found my first job in a factory there, in Baldock.'

Ten

Trials and Tribulations

When I told a friend recently about the way I left home at ten years old for an unknown destination, for an unspecified length of time, she was noticeably chilled; she rubbed her upper arms as though a cold wind had blown through the room. 'My youngest is ten', she said, shuddering, 'I can't imagine letting her go off like that. I don't think I could do it.' 'You would,' I assured her, 'if the circumstances were dire enough.' She nodded, but she was hardly persuaded.

One would hope, as our parents hoped when they made that sacrifice to send their children away – some as young as three and a half years old – that their trust in the authorities and in the receiving families would not be violated. Generally, children were treated decently but, as the foregoing stories have shown, some were not fed well and some were verbally abused because of their ethnicity.

While Manning M's story exposes the appalling fact that some evacuees were malnourished, even starved, by their hosts, this was rare among the people that I interviewed. Most of them as children, even though they were often unhappy and frequently treated as servants or farm hands, were usually given enough to eat by their hosts. Archives from the Imperial War Museum in London, however, indicate that maltreatment of evacuees was as not rare as might have been hoped and that sometimes the neglectful or harsh treatment came not only from hosts but also from figures in authority.

A file from the Ministry of Housing and Local Government – 'Closed until 1972' to the public and to researchers – contained several original letters, hand-written and typed, from mothers and fathers who found the billets for their children far from satisfactory.

Letters told of a room being needed by the host's daughter, leaving the evacuee without a billet and not knowing where to go. Some evacuees, their parents wrote, slept on the floor, some slept on a landing where three children shared one three-foot wide bed, two children at the top and one at the bottom. The letters told of the foster mother being out all day, of children having no hot midday meal, of being fed only sandwiches, of being completely unsupervised, of becoming verminous. Parents did not want their children to return to possible danger but they had to bring them home. In a number of cases, doctors then found the children suffering from malnutrition.

The case of two brothers, Reginald and Douglas Rimmer, ages thirteen and eleven, is particularly chilling. The boys were evacuated from Tooting Graveney School in south-west London, to Maudlin in Chichester, West Sussex, to a Mrs Reed. Soon after their arrival in October, they contracted impetigo and scabies and they became patients at Wick House Hospital. They were in the hospital for nearly six months. When their mother heard that they were ill, she travelled to Maudlin immediately. She was allowed to see her boys only on sufferance – because she had made the journey – and was warned by the Matron in most officious terms that she would not be allowed to see them again, even if she made the journey. She was informed that reports would be sent to her and she would be advised if the children had a relapse.

The children, the mother wrote, were smothered from head to foot in a rash and sores and they looked very ill and pathetically fragile. Neither parent had the opportunity to see them again in hospital. In February, the boys were sent to a new billet in Sidlesham, to a Mrs Franks. They still had sores. They did go to school but they were isolated at the back of the classroom. The boys' condition relapsed and they went back into hospital, this time to Ichener Hospital, where they were treated with sulphur baths. Their parents were allowed to visit and the boys were finally returned to Mrs Franks' house where they seemed happy. Everything was satisfactory until Whitsun, 1941. The boys' mother helped Mrs Franks out with food and other items; she was eager to make the evacuation of her two sons a success, but Mrs Franks had family problems. She was in financial difficulties – and then her unmarried daughter returned from the services pregnant. The mother confined her daughter to a bedroom for the remainder of the pregnancy until after the birth – to 'maintain the good name of the family.'

Mrs Rimmer worried about her two sons under these circumstances. They seemed happy – and the Rimmers didn't think they should return to London and the dangers of the time. It turned out that the boys were substantially undernourished, Reginald developing tubercular glands of the throat. Their ration books had not been fully used, the meat ration, particularly. Could the Franks not afford to feed the children properly, the Rimmers wanted to know, and why were the boys allowed to become so unhealthy? Who was supervising?

In Richard Titmuss's *Problems of Social Policy*, his study of the Second World War, he writes that the arrival of millions of evacuees in country areas where social services had not reached the same degree of development as in the towns from which they came did create a bit of discontent and disorganization. For the Rimmer family, the neglect and maltreatment of their children implied more than a 'bit' of disorganisation.

'Jews are heathens!' 'Dirty Jews!' 'Jew!' 'I don't know how those Jew kids are dragged up!' All of these epithets, and more, were hurled at the Jewish evacuees whose stories are told here, and one might have thought that anti-Semitism was a relatively new phenomenon in British life, dating back, perhaps to the huge influx of Eastern European immigrants at the turn of the twentieth century.

Anti-Semitism in Britain, though, has a long history. Jews are known to have arrived in England in 1066 with William the Conqueror. He invited a group of Jewish merchants from Normandy to join him, thinking their commercial skills and capital would make England more prosperous. Jews, however, were not permitted to own land or to participate in trades. They were primarily limited to money-lending for interest – an activity considered a sin for Catholics.

The history of Jews in Britain is of alternate acceptance and rejection. During Henry I's reign (1135-1189), a Royal Charter treated Jews as though they were the King's own property. Jews were permitted to move about the country, to buy and sell property. They also gained the right to be sworn on the Torah rather than on a Christian Bible.

During this period, Jews contributed heavily to the treasury. All property obtained by usury, whether by Jew or Christian, fell into the King's hands on the death of the usurer and during this time, Jews lived on good terms with their non-Jewish neighbours. By the end of Henry's reign, however, they had incurred the ill-will of the upper classes. The crusades, towards the end of Henry's reign, spread anti-Jewish sentiment throughout Britain.

The years 1189-1190 saw violent and deadly attacks against Jews in London and in York. When Richard I was crowned, several of the most high-ranking Jews arrived to honour him at Westminster, but there was objection to Jews being present at such a holy ceremony. A rumour was started that the King had ordered a massacre of the Jews and a mob set fire to the houses of Jews and killed all those who tried to escape. Similar riots followed at Stamford Fair on 7 March 1190 and on 18 March, fifty-seven were slaughtered at Bury St Edmunds. The Jews of Lincoln were able to save themselves by finding refuge in a castle.

Further attacks on Jews occurred in Colchester, Thetford and Ospringe, but perhaps the most memorable event occurred in York on 17 March 1190. The Jews of York, alarmed by the massacres and fire-settings by anti-Jewish rioters, asked the warden of York Castle to receive them and their families and they were accepted into Clifford's Tower. The tower, however, was besieged by a mob of crusaders demanding that the Jews convert to Christianity and be baptized. Their rabbi advised them to kill themselves rather than convert. This event is reminiscent of the siege of the fortress of Masada, near Jerusalem, where in the year AD 73, the Zealots, Jewish rebels against the Romans, committed suicide rather than surrender their beliefs. At York Castle, the father of each family killed his wife and children and then the rabbi stabbed all the men before killing himself. The few Jews who did not kill themselves surrendered to the crusaders on a promise that they would not be harmed, but they were also killed.

Jews were increasingly persecuted in the 1200s as their contributions to the treasury became less significant and petitions were sent to the King to remove his Jews from the boroughs. They were expelled from city after city throughout the thirteenth century. Those who remained were the chattels of the King. In 1290 the King issued a decree that all Jews should be expelled from England. They could take only what they could carry. They did not formally return until 1655 and there is no official record of Jews on English soil, although some Jews remained clandestinely, practicing their religion in secret.

Towards the middle of the seventeenth century, a small colony of Jews from the Netherlands, Spain and Portugal – Sephardic Jews – settled in London, allowed to re-settle by agreement of Oliver Cromwell. Not that all were in favour; there was some vehement opposition by the more conservative elements, as well as some welcoming sentiments expressed by Quakers and others.

Henceforth, Jews gradually gained acceptance as well as civil rights. In 1837, Queen Victoria knighted Moses Haim Montefiore, and four years later Isaac Lyon Goldsmid was made Baronet, the first Jew to receive a hereditary title. The first Jewish Lord Mayor of London, Sir David Salomons, was elected in 1855, followed by the 1858 emancipation of the Jews. In 1858, the law restricting the oath of office to Christians was changed and Lionel de Rothschild was finally allowed to sit in the House of Commons; Benjamin Disraeli, a baptized Christian of Jewish parentage, was already a Member of Parliament who, in 1874, became Prime Minister. Since 1858, Parliament has never been without Jewish members.

From the 1880s through the turn of the 1900s, a huge influx of Jews to Britain occurred as a response to the massive pogroms in Russia.

By 1919, there were about a quarter of a million Jews in Britain, most of whom lived in the large cities, especially in London. They settled primarily in the Spitalfields and Whitechapel areas, making the East End a largely Jewish neighbourhood. They also settled heavily in Manchester and Salford and everywhere generally embraced assimilation into the wider English culture. By the 1930s, there were some 350,000 Jews in Britain. Some 50,000 Jews had served in the Armed Forces during the First World War, and about 10,000 died on the battlefield.

There was some highly visible anti-Semitism in the 1930s, particularly by the British Union of Fascists, formed in 1932 by the 'aristocratic adventurer' Sir Oswald Mosley. The British Union of Fascists made a considerable impact, with its full-time blackshirted Defence Force, its aristocratic and Tory sympathizers and, for a time, the backing of Lord Rothermere and the *Daily Mail*. It spread its fascist message through demonstrations and a range of publications. Its membership soon numbered about 40,000, winning young people looking for action by linking the woes of the time: unemployment and poor living conditions. The East End of London became his focus because in 1936 a large percentage of Britain's Jews lived there. Mosley's East End campaign began in the summer of 1936 with a huge rally in Victoria Park. Then followed activities that mirror those of Adolf Hitler of the time: fire-bombing and smashing the windows of Jewish shops, racist abuse and physical attacks. This was to be followed by a massive march through the East End, a show of strength designed to intimidate labour and communist organizations and, particularly, the local Jewish community. Mosley planned to send thousands of marchers through the East End of London dressed in the uniforms styled on those of the Blackshirts, much like those worn by the Nazis in Germany. The event has become known as The Battle of Cable Street.

The Board of Deputies of British Jews saw the march as Jew-baiting and urged Jews to stay away. The Communist Party of Great Britain initially also tried to stop is members from participating. None of these groups heeded the warnings. Violence was expected but even so, the government refused to ban the march and a large escort of police was sent – not to prevent the march but to prevent anti-fascist protesters from disrupting it!

The march did not take place as planned because the anti-fascist groups erected roadblocks to prevent the marchers from entering the streets. Police – up to 10,000, according to the *Daily Herald*'s estimate – clashed with the hundreds of thousands of anti-fascist demonstrators but the police could not clear the way for the marchers. 'They shall not pass' was the rallying cry. The British Union of Fascist marchers were dispersed towards Hyde Park instead – a triumph for those opposing the evils of fascism and racism.

The outcome was the passage of legislation to forbid the wearing of political uniforms in public and which required police consent for political marches. It also led to a sharp decline in the ranks of the British Union of Fascists.

Many of the evacuees, young as they were, had heard of Oswald Mosley and had a vague idea of what he stood for, but they, themselves, had not experienced anti-Semitism until they were away from home among strangers. There, long-standing, latent antagonism against Jews was exposed.

Eleven

Henry C's Story

Henry, thirteen years old, and his little brother, Frank, aged seven, were evacuated from Willesden with their school, much like all the other children who left home on that morning in early September, 1939 but, unlike any of the other people I interviewed, this was not the first time these children had packed their little suitcases and boarded buses and trains headed for unknown destinations. Also unlike the others, they were never to see their parents again.

The previous chapter on trials and tribulations sets out a brief history of anti-Semitism in Britain. Over the centuries, violence against Jews waxed and waned, at times flaring up into murderous assaults and, more than once resulting in decrees to oust all the Jews from the kingdom. Never though, was violence perpetrated against a people on the scale we were to see in the 1930s and 1940s in Germany.

Henry and Frank were Heinrich and Franz when they disembarked at Harwich early in 1939. They were participants in the *Kindertransport*, a rescue mission to save some 10,000 children, mainly Jewish, from the violent attacks of the Nazis. Only a few months before, Kristallnacht had been staged – the pogrom instigated by the Nazis in which more than 200 synagogues were destroyed, thousands of Jewish businesses were vandalized or looted, countless windows of shops and homes were smashed, and at least ninety people were killed.

'My mother and father never dreamed that we would be victims of any kind,' Henry told me. 'Our family was thoroughly German, had been in Germany for generations and were completely assimilated. We didn't even think of ourselves so much as Jews, but rather as Germans.'

The boys' father was a successful businessman who owned his own manufacturing company and, with his wife, participated in the social life of Berlin. They attended concerts and the opera, served on the boards of various arts institutions, and were known for their philanthropy. They had mostly non-Jewish friends, but those friends gradually distanced themselves as association with a Jewish family became suspect – and dangerous.

'We were fortunate to leave with the Transport when we did. We had to go via the Netherlands because the Nazis wouldn't allow the transports to leave from German ports. The last transport supposed to leave the Netherlands arrived there just after the Dutch surrendered to Germany. The boat could not leave and those kids were trapped; they were later murdered by the Nazis.'

A variety of organizations – Jewish, Quaker and Christian groups of many denominations – participated in the rescue operation, providing funds and finding sponsor families for the children. Henry and Frank, who soon anglicized their names, were the guests of a Jewish family in North London who welcomed them into their home.

'The Sharps told us, after we'd been with them for a few weeks, that they could hardly restrain their smiles when they saw us because we looked so foreign. We dressed ourselves in the few clothes we had brought with us and they were short trousers, trimmed with buttons, and long socks. They immediately took us shopping and they bought grown-up, ankle-length trousers for me, and plain shorts for my brother that he wore with short socks. They were good to us and wanted us to feel as though we belonged.'

Still, almost before they had settled in with the Sharps, they were caught up in 'Operation Pied Piper' and sent off to the country.

'My little brother was particularly upset at this second move. There had been so much turmoil in his life, already, and he missed our mother so much. He was not much more than a baby, really. Then, that business of being picked out by people… the pointing of fingers, "this one, that one", it was frightening. On what basis were they choosing? Would we be shunned if they knew we were German? If they knew we were Jewish?'

They were chosen by a family willing to take the two boys together and they were treated well, although the school was shared with the village children and class time was limited. Despite that, they learned to speak English quickly, and Henry, as a grown man, spoke in cultured cadences, with only the merest trace of a foreign accent.

'They gave us food that was quite good, I think, and there was plenty of it, but we had never tasted such dishes before. I did not know what Shepherds' Pie could be – did they actually cook shepherds?' He laughed. 'Or Bubble and Squeak, or Welsh Rabbit that had no rabbit in it… That was an education in itself.'

After about a year, when the Blitz began, the boys' host family in Willesden decided to leave the danger zone for the small town of Burgess Hill, about ten miles from Brighton in West Sussex, and the children left the evacuation area to be reunited with the Sharps.

After leaving school at fourteen, Henry apprenticed with a large catering company in London, spending all his lunch hours reading on the back steps of the hotel building. He was determined to educate himself, he told me, so that he would have some skills beyond the three R's.

'I volunteered for the army as soon as they would take me. I had reason!' he emphasized, pursing his lips. By this time, he had learned from his father, who had escaped from Germany and was living in Argentina, that his mother had been captured by the Nazis and had perished in the gas chambers. Soon after Henry discovered his whereabouts, his father, whose health had been seriously undermined by the traumas of his life, also died. Henry did well in the army, soon moving through the ranks of commissioned officers to become, finally, a captain.

'Perhaps I was advantaged by being fluent in German,' he surmised. Somewhat cryptically, he added, 'It had its uses.' I tried asking him a couple of questions in my schoolgirl German, struggling to put the words into coherent sentences. He answered in English. 'I don't care to use German any more,' he explained. 'I'm English, now. English is my language!'

After the war, he became a British citizen. Frank, his brother, moved yet again, emigrating to Israel in the 1950s.

Twelve

Helen Onfong's Story

Helen was twelve years old when she was evacuated from the Lavender Hill School for Girls, in Wandsworth, in South-West London. A soft spoken, elegantly attired woman, she told her story eagerly, the words spilling fast, falling over each other, as though she had been waiting to reveal the details for a long time. Her home just before the onset of the war was in Clapham Common.

'It was September the first, 1939, when we went away. Actually, we were at the seaside on holiday and there was an announcement on the wireless saying that children must return home in preparation for the evacuation. We went home straight away and then we were told to go with our school so we trotted down to the school, my sister and I – we both attended the same school – with our gas masks and our suitcases that my mother had packed for us. I remember her saying that she didn't know what to put in the bags, exactly. She decided on just a few essentials as no one knew how long we would be away. My mother didn't come with us as there were strict instructions that no one was allowed to see us off. She just waved us goodbye from our front door.

We walked to the station from the school to board the train. I think we went to Battersea Station. No one knew where we were going, what our destination was. It turned out that we were on our way to a place called Liss, in Hampshire, that's on the way to Portsmouth on the South Coast. Now I think about it, Portsmouth is a naval town and it was extensively bombed during the war and many houses were destroyed. I've heard that they still occasionally find unexploded bombs there. Still, that's the region where they saw fit to send us – and I don't think there were any air raids in or near Liss when we were there. It seemed a long time on the train, at least three hours, but it couldn't have been that long, really. And on the way, we were given a brown paper bag with an apple, an orange, and some biscuits. Oh, and in the bag there was also a card to post to our parents when we got to wherever we were going.'

'*Can you remember how you felt about going away?*'

'I remember feeling it was terrible. I had to leave my mother and my family. I know that it has followed me all my life, that experience of being torn away from home in such haste. A kind of melancholy, is the only way I can put it. It sometimes awakens me in the night, and I wake up with this kind of heavy feeling in my chest, a kind of dread.'

'*Tell me what happened when you got to Liss. How were you billeted?*'

'Well, we were all assembled in the village hall. Somebody from a village family brought a car to pick us up. We were picked rather quickly, three of us – my sister and I and a friend of ours. The people seemed to want to take us, and we think it was because we were dressed rather nicely. My mother followed the Royal family's children. She read all about them in the newspapers and women's magazines, and she dressed us like the princesses. We were about the same age as Elizabeth and Margaret.

We were taken in the car to a grand house belonging to very wealthy people. I suppose you could call them gentry. But we didn't stay with them, in their part of the house, nor did we see much of them. We stayed with the servants. There was a cook, a butler and a gardener. We ate with the servants in the kitchen. It was the cook, really, who looked after us. She was an older lady, very kind, and she would take us into town on market day. We'd enjoy that. The house was four miles from the school and we walked there and back every day.

My sister and I were at that house for about six months, although our friend left much sooner. She was so homesick and she sobbed bitterly all the time and she stopped eating, she was so miserable. Then, eventually, the lady of the house went on war duty and we had to leave. We were sorry to go as we quite liked it there. If we couldn't be at home with our family, this was as good a place to be as we could imagine.'

'*And what happened to you then?*'

'Well, we were sent to several different places. We seem to have been constantly packing our things and going somewhere else. But after that first place, which was really nice, it was downhill all the way. At the second place there were two old ladies and we didn't stay there long. I think I was there for six months or so. Actually, my sister left first and went to another place. The people weren't used to children and they couldn't cope with two young people, so we two girls were separated for a while. The next place, the third place – I lose count – the third place we didn't like at all.'

'*Why, were you not treated well?*'

'I can't really say that we were treated well. It was horrible there. The people had seven children and they were very religious – Baptist, I think – and our family was Church of England. There was a living-in maid and she and the husband of the family, the father, did all the cooking.' Helen lowered her voice at this point and whispered, 'Do you want to know the sordid details?'

'*Tell me whatever you think I should know,*' I said.

'Well, it seems that the man and the maid had a baby together. It was an uncomfortable situation for us girls, pretty shocking, especially as the man had his eye on me. I was a big girl by now, with a developing figure. My mother discovered the man's interest in me, the way he ogled me, when she visited us one weekend and she immediately made the effort to get us transferred to a more wholesome place. She was concerned about the circumstances, even though the people were so religious, quoting scripture from morning to night.'

'*Did things get better when you moved to the fourth place?*'

'No, unfortunately not. We just slid further downhill. The house was dirty and the food they gave us was inedible, really. I think they'd had several sets of evacuees before us and they were pretty tired of it. Then my sister went on to a higher school, and that's when I came home.'

'*When you got home, did you find yourself caught up in the bombing?*'

'By the time I got back to London, we had already been bombed out and we were living in another house. Our house was completely demolished, blown to bits. My grandfather lived next door to us and the bomb dropped in the garden of his house and pulled down the backs of both our houses. I was not there at the time, of course, but just seeing what was left of our house – the windows all blown out and shattered, the rubble of bricks, the furniture in splinters, was very upsetting. Yes, the bombing was very severe then, and then came the doodlebugs – the buzz bombs – and, yes, it was very frightening.' She shook her head, saddened by the images she was conjuring.

'*I suppose you spent a lot of time in shelters at this time?*'

'Actually, no. My mother refused to go down into the shelter. She always kept a stiff upper lip. "If we are going to die," she'd say, "we'll do it in our own home, in our own beds". So we stayed indoors.'

'*How long were you away from home altogether?*'

'You know, I get confused about that. I think it was between two and three years, altogether.'

'*You were at a fairly good school when you went away. What can you say about your education during the evacuation?*'

'It was bad. It was definitely bad because I didn't finish my schooling. I did go to night school when I came back to London and things had settled down a bit.'

'*Why didn't you finish school? What do you think was the reason for your education being so curtailed?*'

'There were too few teachers to deal with all the extra children. The village school was there to serve the villagers so maybe we had two hours a day in school. I think the village children were also short changed. It must have been resented. The fact is, though, we missed so much school time, I didn't think any of us could ever catch up.'

'*Were you a fairly contented kid when you were away from home?*'

'No, I wasn't! After the very first house we stayed in, I was very unhappy. I cried constantly. I hated being away. I was just one miserable girl. As I said, I've been negatively affected by the experience for the rest of my life – not only being so unceremoniously taken from home and sent into the unknown, as it were, but also being in London when bombs were falling – seeing our house in ruins, waiting for the buzz bombs to land… There was a terrible precariousness about it all, and I still feel insecure and nervous.'

Thirteen

Joan Martinez's Story

'I know we were all excited because we were told we were going away to the country on a holiday. We were told we would be going for two weeks and that we may come back after that two weeks. I remember some of the things that happened when I was evacuated but, for some reason, I don't remember much at all about actually being evacuated. I don't even remember the actual date but it must have been a couple of days before the day that war was declared. Let me see what I can recollect…'

'I was about ten years old at the time and I lived in North Acton, in the County of Middlesex, very close to London. I went to Acton Wells School, a London County Council school, and that's where all the children gathered. From several schools, I think. We were knitted together with various other children and lined up in pairs and put on buses. We left from the Great Western Railway station in Acton, each with a small amount of luggage. Our little gas masks were hung around our necks, and we were told what to do if we ever needed to use them. I remember that we had fitted them to our faces when we first got them some time before, making sure to tighten the straps at the back so nothing – no gas –could seep in. Of course that meant no air could get in at the sides, either, only through the filter thing at the front. Mine was horribly uncomfortable. Thank goodness, we were never called upon to use them. My mother and my aunt came to the railway station to see us off, and we were put on this big train and we ended up in Plymouth in south Devon. I don't remember the ride at all.

From Plymouth, we were then transported to a small village called Ermington. We were gathered together in the local school hall and – it was a terrible situation – barbaric really now that I think about it because we were picked out like little animals, "I'll have this one, I'll have that one, and I'll have those". And, unfortunately, the little girl that I was paired with started crying. She was younger than me and I tried to comfort her, but she was very upset, tears dripping down her face. Because she was sniveling, poor little kid, no one wanted to take her and she was my partner, so I think we were the last to be chosen.

It was a really upsetting thing to stand there and have people pick you out. I guess I had been spoilt. Nothing like this had ever happened to me before – to wait to be picked out, to keep being passed over as though we weren't good enough. I don't remember all that much about that day but I'll remember that part of it forever.

At last, we went with this elderly couple, a lady and her brother, to their little cottage. I think we were treated quite decently in both the places we went to but we weren't at all happy at this first place. The cottage had no electric lights, of course, just candles, primus stoves, and oil lamps, none of which we were used to, coming from a developed urban area. It was a very dark and dismal place; neither of us like it there, not the other little girl nor myself. The food was terrible that the lady prepared for us. To us, it was terrible anyway, as kids. We thought it was awful. Lots of sloppy porridge kind of stuff, and meat minced up, also sloppy. We'd never tasted anything like it in our lives before. And the people weren't used to children. They put us to bed very early – to get rid of us, I think. They had no ideas about what to do with us. At home, of course, we would have listened to the wireless or played records – but with no electricity we were hard put to it to think of anything to do. We were at that cottage for about three months, when the teachers at school realised we were not happy there and they moved us to a farm.

We just loved it at the farm. We had all the food we wanted, good food, because the lady exchanged some of her butter for some meat from the butcher. It was a sort of barter system, I suppose. We had a wonderful time there. I mean, we worked. We didn't sit around, even as kids. I mean we might have sat around at home but we didn't sit around there. We worked. We washed dishes and floors, we went out and fed the chickens, we milked the cows and fed the calves. But I enjoyed it so much because it was entirely different from anything I had done before. I really loved it in the country. The air smelled so sweet. Even I, as a child, enjoyed that aspect. Eventually, though, Mavis, the other little girl, who seemed happy to be there at first, became so miserable that the farm people had to send her home. She never really got over her homesickness. She cried herself to sleep every night and I didn't know how to make her feel any better. So then I was there by myself, until my mother and my little brother joined us and we were a family again – except for my father. He would come down to see us often as he could. Before that, my mother and the baby had been evacuated to Torquay while my father stayed in London. Our home in London was bombed twice and my father had to live in digs. He had to stay in the city because he couldn't be released from his war work.

When she joined me at the farm, my mother helped the lady of the house with chores. We were quite a crowd, then: the lady and her husband, her daughter and, later her son and daughter-in-law, my mother, my baby brother, and me. My mother was quite happy there. She seemed to enjoy country life, too, and she appreciated all that the folk there did for us. They were good, kind people.'

'*Can you recall what kind of schooling you had during this time in the village?*' I asked her.

'Well, for some reason, I don't know why, we never sat that exam at age eleven. I did take the primary exam in Acton Wells before I left home. In Ermington, we were in the little village school and I never sat any type of examination at all. Perhaps they weren't on the same system as London. I just don't know. It was just a regular school. We did the three R's, and not much else, sharing the school with the local children. We weren't popular there at first, until they got used to us. We were intruders, after all, and the school was quite crowded. I left school at fourteen. We eventually came back to London and I went to work there.'

'*So not having taken the second part of the examination was a serious detriment to your opportunities for education?*'

'Yes, it really was. Later, my father paid for me to go to business school so that I could do office work, secretarial work, rather than go into a factory or into a retail shop. I don't think I would have liked that.'

'*How long were you in the Plymouth area altogether?*'

I don't really remember exactly. I think it was about three years because from there I left for Southampton, which was like going from the fat into the fire, and we stayed there with relatives.'

'*Did you have any experiences of the bombing yourself?*'

'Oh, yes. We had three nights of heavy bombing of Plymouth, itself, and it was completely razed to the ground. The lady I stayed with – it was such a sad situation – her son and daughter-in-law had gone into Plymouth one evening to the theatre. When the air raid began and the bombs started falling, they were told by the management that they could not stay inside the theatre. They had to go and stand outside. So they stood by the big columns and during that time a bomb fell and, although they were standing out there with their arms around each other, the son was blown away and they never saw him again. The couple had their arms around each other yet he was just blown away! It was just unreal.'

'*And that was the place you were sent for safety!*'

'Well,' she grimaced. 'I guess no place was really safe. I've heard that if the Germans had any bombs left in their bomb bays after a raid, they just emptied them randomly over the countryside as they returned to their bases. Nowhere was safe. When you look at a map of England and see how small it really is and how close the countryside is to the cities, it's a miracle that some areas actually never experienced any kind of bombardment at all.'

'*How did your family fare back home during this time?*'

'Not too well, actually. As I told you, our house was bombed out twice. The first time the house was bombed, my mother and father had to go across to the church and sleep there the night, with other people from the neighbourhood whose houses were no longer habitable. The second time, they had to go down into the Underground. They couldn't stay in the church that time because bombs were dropping all around that, too. My mother and my baby brother and my aunt and her little adopted brother all went down and slept in the Underground, on the station platform. That was a terrible time for them, sleeping on the platform with hundreds of other people and with a baby, too. I've always wondered if anyone ever rolled onto the electric lines – they were so close to where the people were sleeping, but I never heard that that happened. And trains would come through and stop and people would get off and have to step around the people sitting and lying on the platform, taking shelter. What a nightmare that must have been! Then, not a moment too soon, my mother and the baby were evacuated to Torquay, until they joined me at the farm.

Eventually, we went to Southampton for a while where my mother was needed to help with a family member who was ill. Southampton was certainly not a safe area, being a major port. We all returned to London towards the end of the war, when our house was repaired. Unfortunately, while it stood empty, the house was looted and everything was stolen. We lost all our china and silver. Even the cup hooks were gone! I suppose that was a minor cost of the war, considering that we all came out of it alive, but it was pretty shocking at the time. It's hard to believe that people could be so horrible as to loot a bombed-out house.'

Fourteen

Rosemary Beard's Story

Rosemary spoke with a delightful Welsh lilt so I was a little surprised when she told me that she came from the south of England.

'We lived in Seven Kings at the time we were evacuated. That's about fifty miles the west side of London, near Ilford. I was seven years and a few months of age, as was my twin sister. We went away with hundreds of other evacuees. The 1 September 1939, it was. I remember the journey very well. We were put on a double-decker bus at our school and I can remember our mother travelling on her bicycle, and she tried to keep up with the bus for as long as possible. When the bus gathered speed, she just couldn't keep up any longer and she fell further and further behind – and the look on her face, to this day, still haunts me.

We arrived at Seven Kings Station and we walked down a lot of steps. I can remember that my case was rather heavy for me and a policeman came and took the case from me and helped me.'

'Can you recall anything about the time just before you went away?'

'The evening before we were evacuated, our mother was packing our bags and I can remember us sitting one each side of her and she was telling us to be good little girls and to help the lady of the house. My mother was a widow and she had always been very strict with us. She told us it was important that we be good girls, and we were to be helpful. She repeated that message several times.'

'You were very young at the time, but what else do you remember about the day of the evacuation? What happened when you got to your destination?'

'Well, our first place of evacuation was on the East Coast, a little town called Whitten, near Ipswich. We travelled all day in the train. I don't recall too much about the school we were taken to but I do remember we stayed with a family of ten children and those people were very kind to us. We were there for just six weeks. We never went to school and I remember that it was glorious summer for six long weeks and it was like we were on a wonderful summer holiday.'

'*So you were moved from the first place, which you rather liked – except it was very crowded, I gather – and then taken to a second place. Can you say anything about that place?*'

'The second place we went to was in Ipswich, We were there for approximately seven months. They were a middle-aged couple and the woman's mother was staying with them. This was to be a very unhappy experience for the two of us. Although we were just seven years of age, we were expected to do all the house cleaning, to set all the meals, and to wash up all the dishes. Mr Grimsby, the man of the house, used to check up on us after we had done the dishes to see that they were clean and dry to his standards. And on Saturday, we had to clean the house from top to bottom. We had to dust and polish the furniture, brush the rugs and wash the kitchen and bathroom floors. Can you see just us – two little girls, on our knees, with our hands in buckets of hot water, wringing out cloths and swabbing the linoleum!'

  'Another job we were assigned was to gather up the empty beer bottles and go to the local public house, which was not too far away from the grocery shop. The husband and wife were both beer drinkers and they told us to go into the back door of the pub with the empty beer bottles and somebody would give us new bottles of beer for us to take back to the house where we were staying. We were told many times "Do not tell anyone that you go to the pub to get the beer." Of course, we didn't know that it was illegal to send children into the public house.'

'*It's clear that you were quite unhappy in this place. Did you tell anyone about this? What happened?*'

'Well, I can remember a teacher coming to the grocery store and she seemed to think we were living in ideal surroundings. She told us we were lucky little girls to be living with such nice people, and I can remember my sister and I thinking to ourselves, what must the other children be going through? We did all the housework and, although the people were not physically cruel to us, we were certainly not happy there.'

'I understand that, then, as a school, you were transferred again. Can you talk about that? Was that a good move for you?' I asked.

On 16 May 1940, which was our eighth birthday, we came home from school and we were told that we were being removed from Whitten, and evacuated again, this time to Wales. We were to leave on the following Sunday. So, once more, we packed our bags. We were up at five o'clock that Sunday morning and we met at the school across the street. We were taken by bus to the train station where, again, hundreds of evacuees were put on a train and we travelled all day. It was a very hot day and we had nothing to eat or drink the whole time. I do remember that. At approximately four o'clock that Sunday afternoon – 19 May, it was – we arrived in a little Welsh town called Maesteg, in Glamorganshire, South Wales.

My memories of that day are very clear. The whole town seemed to be out. People were in the train station and lining the streets. We walked from the station to the school, which was just across the street, about half a block, and we were herded into the building. They gave us all something to eat, I remember, and they tied cards on my sister and me that said "Not to be parted". And I do remember voices saying "I'll have this one, I'll have that one" and a strong voice, the voice of a teacher, I think, said "No, Mrs Jones, you cannot pick and choose." Apparently, Mrs Lewis Jones, who was the surveyor's wife, had come down to see the children and had taken a liking to us two little girls. So Mrs Jones went home without any evacuees.

The other evacuees were all assigned to their various homes – and we still hadn't been placed. One of the teachers, Mrs Madge Lewis, bundled us up in her car and took us to where Mr Richards, the postmaster, and his wife lived. The Richards's had said earlier that they couldn't take two children but that they would take one girl and their neighbour would take the other, if absolutely necessary. Apparently the Richards' changed their minds and agreed to take both of us. Their daughter ran over to Mr and Mrs Lewis Jones' house, not knowing that Mrs Jones had seen us, and liked us, earlier, to tell them about the two girls at their house, and to ask if they would like to come and see us. Mrs Jones recognized us immediately as the girls she had wanted to take, and straight away offered to take us home with her. It was about eight o'clock at night by this time – remember we had been up since five in the morning – when we walked over to Asquin, which was the name of their home, and we were put in the bath straight away. We were two dirty little girls, I do remember, and then we were put to bed.'

'*Were you happy in this billet in Wales?*'

'Oh yes. We were both very happy. Deliriously happy. We didn't realise at the time how fortunate we were to go and live with this middle-aged couple who had no children of their own and who were just like mother and father to us. They were really remarkable people because they opened their beautiful home to us and they treated us like their own children. They were the kindest people we had ever met. We were with them for five years and one month, virtually for the whole war, except for that brief stop at Ipswich, and they always reminded us that we had a mother and they would make sure that we wrote to her and that she, in turn, would come and visit us whenever she could.'

'*Did your mother visit you from time to time?*'

'Well, she would come about every six months – and there's another memory that always comes to me when we talk about my mother. The colliery siren would go off at one o'clock. That would mean that the miners would take their dinner break. And when the siren went off, my mother, who didn't realise what it was, would look up in the sky, thinking that a V1 or a V2 was coming, and her face would change dramatically – until she knew what it was. But I'll always remember that look of absolute terror on my mother's face. Now I know it was because they were under bombardment at home, and they never knew when, or where, those rockets would drop and explode.'

'*Did you girls ever go home during that time, to London?*'

'Earlier, when we were in Ipswich, my sister and I both had the measles and we were admitted to hospital because those people didn't want to take care of us. And on the day we were to come out of hospital, I told the nurse that I had another rash all over me and, apparently, I had scarlet fever. So, I was kept in the hospital for another six weeks and, when I was due to leave the hospital, my mother came and took me back to London. My mother, meanwhile, had been bombed out of her house and she was living with her sister. I do remember the bombs and hiding under the dining-room table when the sirens went. I can't imagine that the table would have offered much protection if the house was hit by a bomb, though I suppose it might have kept the debris off people's heads. But I was only home for about two weeks when my mother took me back to Ipswich to be with my sister. It was the first time we two had ever been parted.'

'How, otherwise, did you feel about going home?'

'Well, I knew horrible things were happening in London, but we were so happy in Maesteg – I'm talking about long after we left Ipswich, of course. We were made aware that there were terrible things happening because a very dear friend's son was lost at sea. And we heard about the bombing. So, while as children we played and had fun and did all the things that kids do, we did realise that what was going on back home was not good for children – and that we were far better off staying where we were.'

'You said the people treated you as their own child and that you felt very much a part of their family. Can you give some examples of that?'

'Well, we used to visit my "aunt's" family in Skewen, which was about fifteen miles away, quite often, and her family always introduced my sister and me as their nieces, and their children treated us as their cousins, but she wasn't really related to us at all. There were lots of adopted aunts and uncles in Maesteg. Welsh people are very friendly and lots of neighbours became unofficial aunts and uncles to the Lewis Jones twins. People took a special liking to us because of the Lewis Jones's and we had all these new family members. To this day, when I write home to those people I met decades ago, I still refer to them as aunts and uncles.

'So, how long were you away altogether?'

'It was from September 1939 until the 21 June 1945 when we returned back to London. On 14 June I had come home from school and had gone to the shop where my aunt (Mrs Lewis Jones) used to buy the groceries, and she looked at me and said "Rosemary, we've had a letter to say that you are going home." I was terribly upset. I couldn't believe it. I didn't want to believe it. I ran all the way to the house and there was the letter on the mantelpiece saying that all the evacuees were being returned on 21 June, back to their homes. We had one week to think about going home. The people in Maesteg were very kind to us. They gave us parties and brought presents. The local Church of England threw a party for us and gave us all Bibles and a cross and chain. The people were very generous to us.'

'*Yours, actually, was one of the happiest experiences of being evacuated that I have heard and, in fact, there must have been few who stayed away for the whole duration of the war. You told me that your whole life was changed by the war. Can you talk a bit more about that?*'

'Well, as you know, my mother was widowed and she had to go out to work. My sister and I were exceptional, I think, because we went back to London for three years after the war and then, when we were close to seventeen years old, an opportunity came up for us to go back and live with the people whose home we were evacuated to. I don't think too many evacuees did that, although they visited their adoptive homes – but an opportunity was made for us to go back and live with the Lewis Jones's, which we did. They had written to my mother, making us the offer and when she saw how ecstatic we were she agreed to let us go. My twin sister became a dental mechanic and I became a nurse eventually, encouraged by the Lewis Jones's. I don't know if I would have become a nurse if I had gone back and stayed in London. We still have many friends in Maesteg. For me, the war changed my life completely.'

'*So, even though you are a Londoner born and bred, you are in fact Welsh by adoption?*'

'Yes, when my sister married, my aunt was very concerned about me so she decided that I should add the name Jones. So I became Rosemary Beard Jones. They were very concerned that I might feel left out. I have long considered myself to be Welsh. When people ask me where I'm from, I very proudly say "I am Welsh by adoption".'

When we think of the price that war exacts from the innocent, we rarely consider the unanticipated costs. While Rosemary noted that her life was changed completely by the war and by being evacuated to the home of loving and caring people, one cannot help grieving for her widowed mother. Peddling her bicycle madly, she had raced behind the bus bearing her children away, eager for every last glimpse of them before they disappeared from her sight – only to lose them, in effect, to another family. Her beautiful little girls, all she had in her life at the time, were away from her for so long that their bonds were severed. When the time and the opportunity came, her daughters chose another family and, thereafter, saw their mother only every couple of years.

Fifteen

My Story, Part Three

I knew that my mother and father had left the big house in Stoke Newington. I knew because the letters they had sent me had the new address written clearly at the top, right-hand corner of the first page. I knew in my mind, but in my heart home was the house I had left, the house where the Portnoys lived, and the Schmidts, where the flights of wooden steps carried me from one welcoming family to another.

'But everyone's gone from there, duck,' my mother explained, trying to ease my disappointment. 'The Portnoys went away to the country. To Buckinghamshire – the whole family. Julius rented a great big, beautiful house on an acre of ground. The man who owns it took his family to America when the war broke out, and Julie took all the Portnoys, and his old mother, as well, to live in that house. We had a letter from them a few weeks ago.' Julius was 'the good catch' who had recently married Ann, the Portnoy's oldest daughter.

'What about the Schmidts? Where did they go?'

'I don't know where they went. They used to talk about their married son in Loughborough, or was it Farnborough? Perhaps they went there. Anyway, they've gone and the whole house is empty.'

My mother was pleased with the new flat in the large block that stood high on the crest of Stamford Hill. For all their married lives, my parents had wanted a council flat, but the waiting list stretched ever longer and their name never got any closer to the top. Now, with so many families gone from London, they had their wish: three bedrooms, a living room, a kitchen and a bathroom, all to themselves – and their own front door.

The flats weren't bad, I had to admit. The lovely big playground was paved with gentle slopes for skaters, and I developed fine skills, wafting along with one skated foot extended behind me, my arms held out at my sides like open wings. My long curls were whipped around my face by the spring breezes as I swooped up and down the un-crowded concrete. None of the schools were holding regular full-time classes, as so few students remained to be served, although children were trickling back to London, as month followed month and the war seemed as far away as ever. I attended classes three half-days a week in a nearly deserted infant school at the foot of the Hill. I knew I wasn't learning much there, but I was left with lots of time to skate, and to read the heaps of books I brought home from the public library.

The announcement came in the post late in May. I had won a scholarship and would start at Skinners' School, a private establishment for girls, in the coming autumn. My Dad congratulated me solemnly and my mother, too, glowed with pride, but it didn't seem to me that I had done anything especially clever. I wasn't even sure I wanted to go to Skinners'.

'Skinners' School for skinny snobs! Na na na, na na na!'

I had often enough joined with my school friends to taunt the girls as they passed by, dressed in their neat uniforms with the red and black bands around their school hats. I had seen the way the girls responded, too. They simply raised their noses in the air, as though something indescribably smelly had invaded their nostrils, and walked quietly away. Besides, Skinners' was evacuated, most of the old school buildings on Stamford Hill transformed into a fire station for the duration of the war. A few rooms did remain open for the girls who stayed in London and, although the staff urged the girls to follow the rules, to wear their uniforms proudly, and to display the good manners befitting their privileges, schooling was a make-shift, part-time affair, even for Skinners' students. The buildings were desolate and neglected, voices and footsteps echoing hollowly along the halls. I went there one day to talk to the deputy head mistress but, despite the teacher's warm welcome and enthusiasm for Skinners', I didn't feel that I was in a school at all.

With the coming of summer, schools closed completely, leaving me total freedom to skate and play and read. The grown-ups in the flats seemed to spend all their time listening to the radio and talking about the war. Every evening, before the news, the BBC played *God Save the King* and followed with the national anthems of all the countries that were occupied by Germany. The anthems of Holland, Belgium, Norway, Denmark, Luxembourg, Poland and Czechoslovakia were played and, on 17 June, when France surrendered, the *Marseillais* was added. Yet, to me, the war still seemed unreal, even when men came and dug great ditches in the grounds of the flats, and built shelters, underground shelters, even though there was nothing to shelter from. Until September.

In September, the skies opened and the bombs started falling. And falling. Every evening, before dark, families left their flats, carrying their bundles and bags of food and drinks, and went under the ground for the night. They fixed up chairs and rough tables and laid ragged rugs on the cold, concrete floors, and each family had its own small territory drawn with invisible boundaries. The sirens wailed with the setting sun and the planes zoomed in before the wailing stopped. No one panicked when the bombs crashed down and the anti-aircraft boomed, although the shelter vibrated with each impact. We children would occasionally open the outer door, taking care to close the dark curtain behind us, to peer into the night lit with flashes, but we were soon drawn back by our parents for fear of flying shrapnel.

My Dad at last found regular work, as an air raid warden, shepherding people into their places in the shelter, settling an occasional argument, making people laugh with his banter, his patter, charming the women and children with his jokes and stories and dazzling smiles, so they forget where they were and why they were there. My mother and I saw little of him. He served five shelters besides ours, and many emergencies called for his attention – a young woman with a burst appendix, another with labour pains – so we had to be satisfied with our small share of him.

My mother loathed the shelter, resenting the closeness of the bodies, the intrusion of others' lives into hers. The heat grew greater as the night passed, despite the cold outside and the chilly dampness of the floor and walls, and the air became heavy and stale. People tried to keep their voices low so that others could sleep, but the crying of the infants, the whispering, the coughing, the grunts and involuntary creature releases around her kept my mother awake most of the night. Odours, too, were powerful, and no amount of disinfectant could stop the smells from the curtained buckets at the far end of the shelter from seeping into the living area.

''N't you asleep, yet?' my Dad whispered on one of his early morning visits to our shelter. Men, women, children lay on the floor, or in deckchairs, or sat uncomfortably upright on old armchairs, sleeping, their mouths open, blankets wrinkled around their bodies, arms and legs flung in awkward positions.

'I wish I was.' My Mum's weariness showed in the rasp of her voice. 'I just can't seem to drop off down here. I've simply got to get to my bed or I won't be able to go to work.'

'But darlin', it's dangerous out there. Lotsa stuff flying about. Stay here for now, there's a good girl, and we'll see what we can do tomorrow.'

After that, we stayed in the flat, in spite of the air raids. My Dad moved the mattress from my bed into my parents' room, and laid it on the floor by the side of the big double bed.

'If we get it, we'll all go together.' My Dad was resigned. He joined my mother and me in the bedroom between alerts, and dragged himself out of a deep sleep when the sirens wailed once more, or when he was called away on an emergency.

By the year's end, the raids became even heavier and the children who had come back to London began to return to the country. One by one, my friends went away and no more classes were held at any of the schools in the neighbourhood. Buildings around us were bombed and crumbled to the ground. Fires blazed, water was scarce and no longer flowed through the taps in the flats. Buckets and bottles, kettles and pots, had to be filled from a public faucet several streets away.

'This is not sensible!' My father was firm. 'I know she doesn't want to go, but we've got to get Monica out of London.'

I began my usual protest at any suggestion that I go back to the country, but was interrupted by my father's insistent, 'Look, Skinners' is in Welwyn Garden City. It's not terribly far away. And you've gotta go to school! That's enough arguing!' One of the teachers at Skinners' was my travelling companion to Welwyn. She helped me with my baggage and settled me into the Jordan's house. I was given a small room on the top floor, a room recently occupied by another, older, Skinners' girl.

'Nasty piece of goods, she was, that Rita,' Mrs Jordan informed me, as I unpacked my case. The woman's long nose quivered with distaste. 'Loose as custard, she was. We couldn't tolerate it a minnit more.'

I tried to listen, but my mind kept going back to the earlier events of the day. It wasn't a long or a hard train ride from London, but I was drained of energy. Leaving Mum and Dad was much harder this time, much harder than before. Now I knew what 'evacuation' meant and I resisted until the last moment.

'Don't send me away!' I begged. 'I don't want to leave you. Don't make me go!' I shouted until I began to cry, and I cried until I made myself sick. 'I'll be a good girl.' I still remember my screams. 'I'll stay down the shelter at night. I'll learn from books. I can learn as much from books as I can from teachers, honest I can! Mum! Please, Mum, I don't want to go. Don't make me go!' Finally, in desperation, my mother smacked me hard across the face with the flat of her hand, shocking me into silence. I was still hiccupping helplessly when the teacher from Skinners' arrived at the flat to collect me.

'And so greedy and lazy, she was,' Mrs Jordan continued. 'I had to ask 'em to take her away and send me someone else.' She eyed my few possessions. 'She didn't have her own face flannel, even. Used ours. I don't know how those Jew kids are dragged up. I really don't!'

The tirade continued to my increasing nervousness. I had almost been persuaded by the gentle teacher who accompanied me on the journey that I would like it here. Should I say I was Jewish? Better not. Not yet.

'Tea'll be ready at five o'clock sharp. The gong'll call you.'

When I heard the metallic booming, I rushed downstairs to the kitchen for a meal of mince and boiled potatoes. The mince was pale brown and very thin. Like diarrhoea, I thought and, although I was hungry, I left most of the food on plate.

'Eat up, Monica!' Mr Jordan encouraged. He seemed kinder than his wife. A policeman by trade, he served as sexton at the church in his spare time.

'She's not like that other one!' Mrs Jordan interjected. 'Never seen anyone pack it away like that Rita. Eat you out of house and home, she would, for the few shillings a week they give you!'

'Forget it, do.' Mr Jordan spoke gently. 'She's gone.'

'You see you finish that good food!' Mrs Jordan turned to me. 'We can't have any waste, here. Finish, or no pudding!'

'That's all right, thank you.' I was trying to hold back my tears. 'I just want to go and write a letter to my Mum and Dad and tell them I arrived safe. They gave me a stamped, addressed envelope.'

'Before you go, you clear the table, miss! Can't get out of it that easy.'

Skinners' School and the local High School shared the same building, the Londoners using the classrooms in the mornings, the Welwyn children using them in the afternoons. On two afternoons a week, my classes were held in a church hall in another part of town. Much of the morning school time was spent in the cloakrooms on the ground floor of the building, practicing air raid drill.

Although few bombers had been sighted in the area, fighter planes sometimes appeared, seemingly out of nowhere. I saw one on my second day at school. I was sitting in class at my desk next to the window on the third floor when a small plane with a cross on its side flew right by me. It swooped so near, I could see the pilot at the controls, goggles and helmet covering most of his face. Then, to my horror, machine-gun fire burst from the plane, sending all the girls scurrying under their desks, as they had been taught. He's aiming at us. Why would he want to do that?

The cloakrooms doubled as shelters and crowds of girls – young women – crowded into the aisles, using the shoe containers as benches and resting their backs awkwardly against the hats and coats hanging behind them. I hated the smell there, musty clothes and perspiration, mostly, and when the singing began, and the girls linked arms and swayed from side to side with the rhythm of the music, I wanted to get up and run away. Not to the Jordan's house. Away.

> We're gonna hang out the washing on the Siegfried Line,
> Have you any dirty washing, mother dear…?

The effort to keep morale high, to unite the girls in a common sisterhood, made me feel more alone than ever. I had no one to talk to. The teachers didn't want to know about my billet – the girls were always complaining about their billets – and even Rita, who used to live with the Jordans, didn't sympathize with me much. 'Mrs J. is a bit of a bitch, I grant you, but the Mister is quite kind, really. Where I am now is much worse, if you must know, so you better put up with it.'

If Mr Jordan were kind, I'd turn to him for support, and try to make the best of it. I smiled at him frequently, and sometimes tried to pretend he was my father. Well, my uncle, perhaps, but it wasn't easy, and it did nothing to stem Mrs Jordan's floods of anti-Semitic abuse. 'Jewish princesses!' she would chide, still unaware of my ethnicity, 'Think they're God's chosen people, they do, but around here they work or they don't eat.'

After only three weeks in the Jordan's house, I was already more miserable than I had been with the Browns towards the end of my stay in Paston. I cried at night, trying not to make a noise, gulping my sobs, burying my face in the pillow, whimpering. The lump in my throat never went away. I was determined to go home.

One morning, before it was light, I counted the money in my purse and, instead of going to school, I went to the railway station, only to find that I was short by fourpence for the fare. I ran to school, borrowed tuppence from Rita and a penny from each of two girls in my class, promising 'I'll pay you back, honest!' and rushed from the school grounds back to the station.

'Half to London, please.'

'King's Cross?' the man in the booth confirmed.

'Er, yes. That's right. Thanks.'

I waited on the platform for the train, eyeing the Nestlés machine. I hadn't eaten breakfast. A penny for a bar. No good. All the money was gone. In the ladies room, to my joy, I found a penny protruding from one of the lavatory door slots. I gradually eased it out with a hairpin and, triumphant, I inserted the coin in the machine, bore the bar of chocolate away, and slowly savoured each delicious crumb.

I thought luck might be with me again at King's Cross, but my careful examination of the doors in the ladies' room there yielded nothing but a suspicious attendant who shouted, 'You clear orf! Ge' away, gel, or I'll call a copper!'

With no money for the bus, I set out to walk from King's Cross to Stamford Hill. The day was nearly gone before I reached the door of the flat, only to find no one home and no way to get inside. I had forgotten that my parents would both be at work. My stomach ached with hunger. Perhaps Dad was at the wardens' post. I ambled through the playground and out into the street, my feet dragging, both from weariness and from the nagging worry I was beginning to feel about how my Mum and Dad would receive me. They weren't going to be pleased. I waited for several moments outside the wardens' post, thinking of the slap my mother had given me, and how my face had stung for ages afterwards, but my fears diminished as my hunger pangs grew more insistent.

I opened the door and peered in. My Dad was sitting there, smoking, and sipping from a big mug of tea. He looked up from the newspaper covering the table and saw me standing in the doorway, my eyes brimming with tears. Without a word, we rushed towards each other, arms outstretched.

'Come on. I'll take you home.' His voice was rough, hoarse. 'You can stay tonight, but you'll have to go back. You can't stay in London. The raids are worse than ever. It's much too dangerous. Mum'll go with you, this time, and find you somewhere better to stay.'

After a night of particularly heavy bombing, when the very foundations of the council estate seemed to rock, my mother took the day off work to take me back to Welwyn Garden City. A talk with the headmistress of Skinners' soon made clear that the woman had little sympathy with me, and still less understanding of what I had experienced.

'We simply cannot condone this kind of behaviour, mother, and we will not recommend another house for her. You must take full responsibility for both her billet and for her well-being. Good day, Mrs Semus.' Politely, but coldly, my mother was dismissed.

Where to start looking? The two of us began our search along the streets near the school, trying to find some clue, some sign, that a house might provide a comfortable, friendly, safe home for an eleven-year-old girl. How could we tell? As we entered a street called, simply, 'The Avenue', we noticed a young woman pushing a pram with one hand, and holding the fist of a small girl of about five years old with the other. The group stopped outside the garden gate of one of the terraced houses where the woman, releasing the little girl's grip, lifted the latch and opened the gate. Pinned to the gate, a hand-painted poster announced in large block letters:

HALDANE SHELTERS. COME AND SEE THE MODEL AT THE
WELWYN STORES ON FRIDAY NEXT

My mother rushed over. She knew about Professor Haldane and
approved of his politics and his plans for safe and comfortable shelters.
These people might be our kind of people.

'Excuse me,' she introduced herself, holding the gate open so that
the woman could steer the pram into the side way. 'I'm looking for
someone who would be willing to take my girl in to live. She goes to
Skinners'. Do you know of anyone?'

The young woman, her long, smooth, corn-coloured hair brushed
straight back off her face so that it swung behind her as she moved,
looked at my mother and then at me, hanging back a few yards away,
and then at my mother again.

'We've got plenty of room.' She hardly hesitated. 'And we'll be
glad to take her. Come in and look around, won't you? I'll make
us some tea.' Over their cups of tea, the two women negotiated the
terms of my stay. All that remained was to collect my clothes from
the Jordans. I really didn't want to go there, but I knew that I must.
I showed my mother the house, remaining in the street while my
mother walked up the garden path to the front door. She knocked.
Waited. Knocked again. An upper window was thrown open and
Mrs Jordan poked out her head. Seeing me standing outside the gate,
she slammed the window shut and made her way downstairs. My
mother waited for the front door to open, almost as nervous as I was.
I could see her hands clenching by her sides. Mrs Jordan appeared in
the doorway with my old suitcase and flung it past my mother onto
the concrete path. She went back into the house, returning after
only a few moments, with a paper carrier bag filled with the rest
of my things. This, too, she threw on the path. The bag burst open,
scattering clothes and papers on the gravel. The front door crashed
shut. Not a word had been exchanged.

I picked up the pyjamas and gym slips and blouses that had been
stuffed, higgledy-piggledy, into the carrier, and folded them neatly over
my arm. Together, my mother and I walked back to The Avenue.

The Scotts were unlike anyone I had ever met. Both Cambridge
graduates, Jim Scott worked as a government economist, travelling to
London by train every day, while Pam Scott was an artist. Her paintings
and drawings hung everywhere in the house, mostly portraits of strong-
faced, tight-jawed men and women, with earnest expressions, grouped
together and facing a shining star. Both the Scotts' university degrees
hung, neatly framed, in the bathroom, over the lavatory.

The house was filled with books, bookshelves fitted into every corner. Books were stacked in the living room, in all the bedrooms, in the baby's room, and even in the bathroom. The Scotts looked at each other strangely, I thought, when I told them I had read some of them – *Romeo and Juliet*, for instance, and they asked me to say what it was about. When I told them, Jim Scott raised his eyebrows in a funny way that made me laugh. He opened his eyes very wide and pretended to stagger backwards in amazement.

'My!' he declared. 'I'm being knocked over wiv a fevver!'

I told them how my mother and I went to the public library every week and filled my mother's big leather bag with books, and when we'd read them, we went back and got another lot. They encouraged me to read more – some books I had never seen before, even in the library. They were Left Book Club editions. The Scotts were communists, they told me, and I thought I knew what that meant.

'Oh, one of my friends' brothers is a communist…' I was eager to please the Scotts, whom I liked straight away. 'He used to go to meetings at Bethnal Green when Oswald Mosley spoke, and once he got his head bashed by some Blackshirts. I'm not sure if Oswald Mosley is a communist…' I stopped, guessing by the Scotts' shaking heads that he probably was not.

Besides work, daily commuting, campaigning for the building of Haldane shelters across the country, and caring for the children, Jim and Pam Scott were part of a group producing the *Daily Worker*. Swearing me to secrecy, they explained that the newspaper had been banned but, because they felt the message of the paper was important, they published a small, mimeographed edition and distributed it to people who wanted it. A printer in town lent them the equipment, and the group clubbed together for the paper and toner. They recruited me to deliver copies of the mimeographed sheet in a shopping basket, and I soon learned the house numbers and the street names without writing them down. I had no idea that what I was doing might be illegal and, certainly, no policeman would suspect a blonde, blue-eyed child of eleven of carrying materials subversive to the war effort. The Soviet Union was friendly with the Nazis and had signed a non-aggression pact with them, but the Scotts explained that it was only a tactic and that the Russians would soon be on our side. It was only a matter of time, they said.

Except for that one lone flyer over the school, the war seemed a long way away from Welwyn, the beautiful, planned garden community, with its wide, tree-lined streets, its open campus, and its elegant stores. Jim came back each evening and told of air raids in London, and the people sleeping on the platforms down in the Underground stations. Both Jim and Pam began to look tired and they sometimes excused themselves from reading aloud to their Jenny and the baby.

'Would you do it instead, Monica, please?' one or other would ask, and I was proud to take their place, making a special effort to act the parts as well as to read them. The whole family loved *Alice in Wonderland* and *Through the Looking Glass* best, even the baby, who chortled and gurgled even more than usual when Lewis Carroll was chosen. I read from those two books until I knew them by heart.

The war seemed a long way away until I heard what had happened to the Lewis Trust Buildings. I knew those buildings from when I lived in Stoke Newington and went to play with my friend, Ruth Berger, whose family had a flat there. Ruth invited me to her birthday party, and all the children had sung,

> A tisket, a tasket,
> A little yellow basket
> I sent a letter to my love and
> On the way I lost it…

Ruth, now a Skinners' girl too, told me that her mother, her father, her grandmother and grandfather, and two of her uncles were there when the gas mains and the water mains burst and almost all the people sheltering from the raid were drowned. 'Caught like rats in a sewer,' Ruth sobbed, repeating what she had overheard one of the teachers whispering to another. 'Rats in a sewer.'

Ruth knew that my father was an air raid warden and begged me to find out if, by some miracle, her parents had been among those saved. I wrote to my Dad, asking him to look on the lists outside the Town Hall. 'If their names are not there, that will be good,' I wrote. My father never answered my question, even though I reminded him several times. I stopped writing about it when one of the teachers took me aside and told me that, although she knew I meant well, it was really not a good idea, not kind, to hold out any hope to Ruth. Everyone in her family was dead. Dead and buried.

The raids on London were now so severe that my parents knew that they must leave the city. One of my father's warden friends recommended Luton, in Bedfordshire, as a good place to live. Plenty of work in the factories there, he said. They both came to take me away from Welwyn Garden City. I felt some pangs of sadness at leaving Jim and Pam, and hugged them both many times, making fervent promises to write. I liked them and the children, especially the baby, but I really was glad to be going with my Mum and Dad. Perhaps I'd be able to stay with them, this time. 'At last, we can be together again, like a family should.' My Dad's throat was tight with emotion. 'I've missed my little girl. I really have.'

The move to another city meant transferring to yet another school, this time to Luton High School, the local private girls' school. My father found work in a factory producing war materials and he somehow managed to pay the fees, my scholarship to Skinners' not being transferable. Luton High was a good school with rigorous standards and I soon felt lost, dimly realizing how much of my education I had missed by being in part-time, occasional classes, and long stretches of not being in school at all. At times, I despaired that I would ever catch up, although I managed to stay at grade level, albeit in the 'B' classes rather than the 'A' stream.

After a year or two, my parents and I returned to London, to yet another flat and, for me, still another school, this time Clapham County Secondary School for Girls, on the edge of Clapham Common. Back in London, my scholarship grant was reinstated.

The heavy bombardment of London had stopped some time before. Instead, now came the buzz-bombs: the V1s and V2s came without warning, without time for sighting, without time to take shelter. One kind announced itself seconds before impact with a slow 'buzzzz, buzzzz, buzzzz.' When the buzzing cut out, we ducked. We threw themselves under desks, tables, any kind of heavy furniture, and waited for the explosion. That was one kind of V-bomb. It was only after the thundering and shattering of windows and the crumbling of masonry that anyone knew the other kind had come.

For a while, no one realised what the explosions were. Gas mains bursting? Could that be it? It was a mystery. The bombs were not dropped from planes; that much was clear. They were fired from across the Channel. Pilotless aircraft, they were called, but they were rockets. No one knew when they would come. We were all on edge.

At school, the 'Matriculation' loomed ahead, the examination that determined whether or not one would go on to university. I knew I could not possibly pass it. Even when I was provided with a tutor for maths, a sixth former of seventeen, I couldn't seem to learn. The moves from school to school, the missed classes, the time spent in air raid shelters rather than in study, all of these left gaps in my knowledge, gaps I couldn't seem to close, because I didn't know what I didn't know. The headmistress was clearly dismayed when I told her that I had found a job and that I would be leaving school. I was fifteen and a half.

'You know you have a legal obligation to stay in school,' she said. 'Your grant was awarded on the understanding that you would complete the course of study.' I didn't say anything. I felt like crying. The Head had always been so nice to me and I never wanted to disappoint her. She shuffled some papers on her desk. 'You have fallen behind in some subjects but you are doing well in others… I gather you show unusual promise in composition… and that you are remarkably well-read for a girl of your…' She hesitated and I was sure she was going to say 'class' but she said 'age' instead.

I still had said not one word, determined not to be lured back into school, so sure was I that I could not succeed. Suddenly weary, the Headmistress briefly rested her head in her hands, and rubbed her eyes. 'All right, Monica, I can see that you have made up your mind,' She rose, as did I, and walked me to the door.

'See that you go to County Hall with your mother or father to sign the necessary papers. You'll probably have to give back some, or all, of the grant, depending on your family's finances.'

Sixteen

Reading, Writing and Arithmetic

For a long time, I nursed my shame at giving up my scholarship, at throwing away such a rare and precious privilege. They had thought me bright enough to benefit from higher education and I had let them down – whoever 'they' might be.

In retrospect, after decades in which to place the evacuation in a larger context, and after talking with dozens of other evacuees, it becomes clear that mine was not a personal failing. It was, rather, the result – perhaps inevitable – of social planning gone awry. Over and over again, interviewees spoke of their part-time schooling. Betty Winehouse and others told of having to teach the younger children because there weren't enough teachers; almost all the children spoke of their limited time in the classroom, and many indicated that their schooling had come to an end the day they left home. One of my acquaintances recently divulged that he had attended thirteen schools during the time he was evacuated, one of them for just one day! Echoing my own insecurities, Helen Onfong left school early because she felt she had missed so much school time that 'I didn't think any of us could ever catch up.' As Irene Sassoon so succinctly summarized – and Joyce Reed confirmed, 'Education was shot to hell!' and, 'My schooling went to pot!'

Clearly, the overriding objective of the evacuation was to remove children from danger areas, from the cities where the bombs were expected to fall from the skies soon after war was declared. Education might be important but, first, let's get the children out of harm's way. One can imagine that this might have been the thinking of the planners. It is instructive, though, to look at both the kinds of education offered in Britain at the time, and at the make-up of the majority of the evacuees.

These days, we take for granted that everybody goes to school. It is not an option (nor was it an option in 1939) and a child's failure to attend school will bring down the full force of the authorities on parents' heads. Even missing more than a few days will raise red flags in the minds of attendance officers.

Compulsory though it is, we think of education as a right rather than a privilege and we wax enthusiastically about the advantages of education as mind-broadening, inspiring, even life-enhancing. We forget that this was not always the case and that universal state schooling well into adolescence is a relatively recent phenomenon, with early roots in the Industrial Revolution. Even so, there were many who didn't approve of educating the masses at all, fearing that 'too much education or schooling would simply make the working poor discontented with their lot'! (Gillard, Ch.2).

Before the nineteenth century there were very few schools, and most of the schools that did exist were run by and for the church, with the emphasis on religious education. Not until 1870 did the Foster Education Act establish compulsory state education in England and Wales, and then only for children aged five to twelve. The Reform Act of 1867 had given the vote to a large number of working class men and it was felt that people needed to be 'educated' if they were to play an informed role in a democratic society. Presumably, being in school until twelve years of age would equip men – and it was just men, then – to cast their votes wisely! Further, with industrialisation and the need for managerial staff, Britain's prosperity would depend on a more educated workforce. It was a matter of national interest to ensure that the population could read, write and compute at some minimal level. Added to this, it was observed that in 1870, Prussia's literate army trounced France's relatively illiterate army – demonstrating that universal education was to be even more in the national interest.

By 1901, the Census Report of that year noted a substantial increase in literacy, but other countries – Britain's competitors, such as Germany and Switzerland – provided a wider range of secondary and technical schools. The message was clear: universal education would be vital to the nation's economic health as well as its political health.

The Balfour Act of 1902 established the basic framework of education that lasted until 1944. Before the changes of 1944 – and the millions of evacuees were included in this group of children – education was guaranteed only until fourteen years of age for the majority of youngsters. There were secondary schools but they often charged fees, so few working class children could attend. Scholarships, such as those my brother and I were awarded, covered tuition and provided grants for school clothing, but such scholarships were provided to only about 10 per cent of elementary school children. Most secondary school students, therefore, were more prosperous middle class and upper-middle class children whose families could afford the fees. Children of the upper class went to public schools. By the early 1940s, there is no question that class-divided secondary schools were failing England's children. Twice as many children were receiving higher education in Germany as in England, more than twice as many in France, three times as many in Switzerland, and nearly ten times as many in the United States.

The Butler Education Act of 1944 established a free national education system and raised the school leaving age to fifteen, with the intention of raising it to sixteen in the future – that did not happen for almost thirty years – and, ultimately, to eighteen years of age.

The educational system prior to 1944 was essentially social class based. Children of the working class were offered limited schooling. They supposedly emerged at fourteen years of age able to read and write reasonably well, with enough arithmetic skills to handle money in, say, a retail shop setting. They were equipped to apprentice to a trade; some went straight to work in factories, learning on the job how to use a sewing machine or a lathe. As Irene S. told her little sister '…we're going home to London, because I'll be fourteen and I'm going out to work to earn a living.' Joyce Reed, Manning M., Joan Martinez and several more of the people I interviewed – as well as countless other evacuees, 'aged-out' of school and returned to the cities when they were fourteen, ready to go to work and 'earn a living.'

These children did not question this reality. If there were options, they did not know about them, they were not encouraged to think about them, and they were, perhaps, not interested in them.

Middle class, upper-middle class and upper class children attended secondary schools and a percentage of them went on to university. To leave school at fourteen and go to work was as unthinkable to them as it was to most working class children that they might attend university.

The majority of those evacuated from the cities to the countryside in 1939 were children of the working class. The more economically secure classes had options: they could, and did, move as families to the countryside; they could, and did, send their children to the colonies or to the United States for the duration of the war, so that their education was relatively uninterrupted. The children who went to the United States would, in fact, have been required to stay in school until they were at least sixteen. (Later on, a kind of lottery was instituted giving a chance to a small number of less affluent children to go to America).

Once they arrived in the country areas, evacuees had to be housed and schooled. Arrangements for billeting, though not always successful, appear to have been made well in advance, the local authorities searching out homes with habitable rooms, but preparations for educating the crowds of children who would arrive in small towns and villages seems not to have been made with the same urgency. Imagine a village with, perhaps, less than fifty children suddenly having to incorporate 200 or 300 new arrivals! We have seen throughout the stories told here that the First World War expedient of 'double shift education' seems to have been used in most places. Children got half-time education at best. Sometimes, no rooms at all were available and classes were held in the open air, or in ill-equipped church halls. Even the children evacuated to Welwyn Garden City with the prestigious Skinners' School, had to share the facilities with the local High School girls. Further, because teachers left the cities with their schools, city schools were closed and children who returned home received no education at all. It should be noted that village children were also deprived of full-time education, which must have caused some resentment towards the evacuees.

It is now generally accepted that the education of working class children before the Second World War was designed less for their benefit than for those who had a vested interest in maintaining their privileged economic and social status. As employees, workers needed to have only enough schooling to perform fairly low-level jobs. During the war, too, educating this group of children was not treated as of first importance but, rather, as an afterthought – a kind of catch as catch can. Nowadays, of course, technological advances have made universal secondary education essential for the nation to provide an increasingly skilled workforce, able to compete with foreign competition.

Afterthoughts…

Fifty years after the onset of the war, I went to visit Benthal Road School, in Stoke Newington, from which I had been evacuated in September 1939. To my dismay, I discovered that it had been bombed and completely demolished during the Blitz. A new, modern school now stands in its place.

It pleases me to note that Skinners' School for Girls, the institution to which I was awarded a scholarship, became a state grammar school under the 1944 Education Act. Fees were abolished and entry is now gained through the Eleven Plus examination, and is based on academic achievement rather than ability to pay.

Seventeen

When All is Said and Done

It has been said that we live twice – once in reality and again when we talk about that reality. In their interviews, people who were children at the outbreak of the Second World War have told their stories of being labelled, lined up, and taken away from their families. In talking about the past, in remembering the events of the times, they both relived and reinterpreted their experiences, realising as adults the full effects of those childhood experiences. For some, the course of their lives was irrevocably changed; they veered off in directions they would never have otherwise taken. For others, the limitations and curtailment of their schooling deprived them of future opportunities, and for still others, the emotional bonds with their parents were seriously weakened.

In hindsight, given what we now know about the year-long 'phoney war', it is possible to see how the planning and the outcomes might have been different. As Titmuss and others have pointed out, the war did not follow the course that the government expected. The physical safety of children from all-out, intensive and prolonged air bombardment by day and night was of first and dominant importance and it was this that shaped the evacuation scheme, this that rushed millions from place to place in the course of a few days. Concern about the psychological effects on the children took second place, compared to the enormous loss of life that was expected if the children remained in the cities.

To be torn up from the roots of home life and to be sent away from the family circle, in most instances for the first time in the child's life, was a painful event. This was no social experiment; it was a surgical rent only to be contemplated as a last resort. The whole of the child's life, its hopes and fears, its dependence for affection and social development on the checks and balances of home life, and all the deep emotional ties that bound it to its parents, were suddenly disrupted. From the first day of September 1939 evacuation ceased to be a problem of administrative planning. It became instead a multitude of problems in human relationships (Titmuss, 109).

It was 'peacetime' for a year before the war began in earnest and the bombers began their nightly raids, yet the street lights were extinguished on 1 September 1939. As Betty Winehouse recalled, 'We went outside; the streetlights were on, and suddenly everything went black. It was a terrible feeling...'. The night was suddenly dark and the 'blackout' prevailed over the entire country from that moment until the end of the war. Not a chink of light was allowed to shine from windows, if torches and flashlights were used at all, they were held down so that light beams shone at one's feet, and hallway lights were turned off when front doors were opened. We got used to the dark streets and alleys, and to the routine of drawing the heavy curtains to black the windows out every evening. And we sang:

> When the lights go on again, all over the world...
> There'll be love and laughter, and peace ever after,
> Tomorrow, just you wait and see.

It was to be almost six years before the lights went on again.

Still, other songs of the time reminded us that this situation would not last forever and that families and loved ones would be reunited eventually:

> We'll meet again, no matter where, no matter when,
> But I know we'll meet again some sunny day.

In the meantime, children were separated from their families, sometimes in settings quite different from their homes. Some of the interviewees, for instance, noted that they were relegated to the 'downstairs' to live with the servants – and this was not only in 'aristocratic' families in grand country houses, as with Irene S. and Phyllis B. but also in the case of Stella Stern, whose host was the local postman. Stella and her sister were treated as total outsiders. Not only could they not eat with their host family but they were also not allowed to participate in family celebrations. One can only conjecture how this kind of exclusion affects young, as yet unformed, personalities.

Domestically, foster parents had little respite from the evacuees, whom the authorities expected to be out of the house from after breakfast until the late afternoon or evening meal, but problems of education complicated this. Perhaps one might extend a modicum of compassion towards hosts who were not used to children or young people and who had little idea of how to involve them in activities or how to keep them entertained. Just as the children had little choice in their billeting, so the hosts, too, were required to accept a child, or children, depending on the number of available rooms in their homes. That might account for, but surely does not excuse, some of the resentment directed against the evacuees.

The evacuation left its mark on many children and in many ways. Bill Reed learned to be competitive – an asset that served him well later in his life; Alan D. appreciated being taken out of a working class family and realizing that there were other paths he might follow; many developed a lasting love for the country; others enjoyed learning about the history of the towns and villages they lived in. Still others were moved around so often that they were left without a sense of belonging anywhere. Some, for the first time in their lives, were made aware that their religion marked them as 'different' and vulnerable to verbal abuse.

In the seven decades since the second 'war to end all wars' began, we who were evacuees in 1939 have reflected on the role of chance in our destiny. Had we been born just twenty-two miles across the English Channel, ours would have been a different and more terrible story, but being torn by the roots from home and moved into strange environments did not leave us untouched or unchanged. Exposure to different ways of living meant worlds of opportunity for some; some were so long removed from their families that they felt like strangers when they returned home.

We remember the evacuation as one of the most significant events in our lives and when we hear of current migrations of children in war-torn lands, we are reminded again of how much the young and innocent must endure through the actions of their elders.

References

Donnelly, Mark, *Britain in the Second World War*. (Routledge, London & New York, 1999)

Gaskin, Margaret, *Blitz: The Story of December 29, 1940*. (Harcourt Inc. Orlando, Florida, 2005) First published in the United Kingdom by Faber & Faber Ltd

Gillard, D., *Education in England: a brief history*. (www.dg.dial.pipex. com/history)

Jackson, Carlton, *Who will Take Our Children?* (940.53161 J.12) (Methuen, London, 1985)

Katz David S., *The Jews in the History of England, 1485-1850* (Oxford University Press, Oxford, 1994)

Price, Richard and Sullivan, Martin, 'The Battle of Cable Street: Myths And Realities'. *Workers News* (March–April 1994)

Titmuss, Richard M., *Problems of Social Policy*. (His Majesty's Stationery Office and Longmans, Green & Co, London, 1950)

Wells, H.G., *The Outline of History, Volume 2*. (Garden City Books, New York, 1961)

Visit our website and discover thousands of other History Press books.

www.thehistorypress.co.uk